INFORMATION TECHNOLOGIES AND SPACE PLANNING FOR LIBRARIES AND INFORMATION CENTERS

INFORMATION TECHNOLOGIES AND SPACE PLANNING FOR LIBRARIES AND INFORMATION CENTERS

RICHARD W. BOSS

G.K. Hall Publishers ● Boston, Massachusetts

INFORMATION TECHNOLOGIES AND SPACE PLANNING FOR LIBRARIES
AND INFORMATION CENTERS

Copyright 1987
by G.K. Hall & Co.
70 Lincoln Street
Boston, Massachusetts 02111

Book production by John Amburg

Book Design by Barbara Anderson

Copyedited by Michael Sims

Printed on acid-free paper
and bound in The United States of America

10 9 8 7 6 5 4 3 2 1

LIBRARY OF CONGRESS CATALOGING
IN PUBLICATION DATA
Boss, Richard W.
    Information technologies and space planning for
libraries and information centers.

    Bibliography: p.
    Includes index.
    1. Libraries—Automation.   2. Library science—
Data processing.   3. Library science—Technological
innovations.   4. Libraries—Space utilization.
5. Library planning.   6. Information services.
I. Title.
Z678.9.B65   1987   022'.9   87–19798
ISBN 0–8161–1859–0
ISBN 0–8161–1870–1 (pbk.)

CONTENTS

Reducing Resistance to Microform
Changing Usage Patterns
Space Requirements
Reading Area
Printing Area
Storage Area
Staff Area

Reliance on Formulas
Formula Revisions Required

1
INTRODUCTION

Library and information center planning has not changed a great deal in the past two decades. The leading published works on facilities planning of the sixties and seventies continue to be widely used and the formulas that provide prescriptions for planning—which are particularly popular in the academic sector—have undergone infrequent and only minor revisions.

A recent major work, *Library Space Planning*, lists the factors affecting library operations that warrant space planning as "lack of collection-growth space, lack of space for people, and a change in the direction or mission of the organization or community served by the library."[1] Information technology is not mentioned as a factor, except for a brief reference to the fact that automating library functions may generate changes in job responsibilities that, in turn, affect space allocation. It is the author's contention that this is a serious omission. Libraries and information centers are changing significantly. More than $200 million a year in equipment is being installed, ranging from automated library systems to the newest optical mass media systems. It is imperative that facilities planning provide for these technologies and for the increasing role that they will play in the future. The technologies influence all aspects of facilities planning: the amount of space, electric power requirements, lighting, furniture design, etc.

This book, which has been written in response to the lack of information about the impact of information technologies on space planning, describes the technologies that have the greatest potential impact, and discusses the facilities planning implications.

Chapter 2 is an overview of libraries and information technologies. It presents a scenario of the library or information center of the future. Chapters 3 through 7 discuss automated library systems, compact storage, microform, optical media, and telefacsimile technologies. The technologies are not all treated in the same way because the space implications of the technologies vary a great deal. An integrated multifunction library system takes much more space than a telefacsimile machine. Microform and compact storage have very different implications. The technologies also differ in their effect on library patrons. Patron access catalog terminals directly affect all patrons, but compact storage in a special collections area may be totally hidden from view.

The emphasis in each chapter is on the aspects of planning and implementation that appear to pose the greatest problems for libraries.

The emphasis in Chapter 3 is on preparing the computer room and accommodating remote peripheral devices, including terminals, micro-based workstations, and side printers.

Chapter 4 discusses microform, still the most widely used nonprint information storage technology in libraries and information centers. The chapter goes into considerable detail on the decision to use microform and the selection of equipment because these are integrally related to space requirements and the most common source of problems.

Chapter 5 discusses optical media, the newest information technologies. Each of the four types is described: videodisc, compact audio disc, CD-ROM, and optical digital disks. It is a lack of understanding about the future role of each of the technologies that appears to be the most serious problem facing libraries.

In Chapter 6, telefacsimile, an older technology that is only now being widely implemented, is discussed. Despite the low cost and small space requirements of the technology, libraries have a considerable number of problems selecting, installing, and operating the equipment.

Compact storage is discussed in Chapter 7. The technology is potentially very effective for storing printed books, journals, documents, and other library materials when additional space is not available, or available only at considerable cost. The emphasis is on structural requirements and the issue of patron access.

Chapter 8 describes the existing space planning formulas

now widely used in facilities planning, and makes specific recommendations for altering them to reflect the changing technologies. Chapter 9 makes specific recommendations for planning facilities that will have to meet the needs of the 1990s.

Note

1. Fraley, Ruth A. and Carol Lee Anderson, *Library Space Planning* (New York: Neal-Schuman, 1985), 1–8.

2

INFORMATION TECHNOLOGIES TODAY

Dramatic changes in information technologies have occurred in the past two decades, especially in the use of library automation and digital telefacsimile. A number of other technologies, among them the somewhat more mundane electromechanical compact storage systems and microform, have also played a significant role in the planning and operation of libraries. The optical media—digitally encoded videodisc, optical digital disk, and CD-ROM—are expected to have a major impact over the next decade.

Automated Systems

While there were fewer than 100 automated library systems in use in the mid-sixties, most of them batch systems operating on IBM mainframes located outside the libraries they served; by the mid-eighties more than 1,000 systems were in use, with a large majority of them based on minicomputers located in the libraries. Not only had a large majority of the nation's largest libraries implemented automated systems by late 1985, but smaller libraries (those with collections of fewer than 100,000 volumes) had installed systems as well. Interest in automation was so great in North America that nearly 7,000 libraries of all sizes were developing archival files of machine-readable records.

The integrated or total systems approach to library automation uses a single bibliographic file to support all functions (acquisitions, serials control, circulation, etc.). While this approach was philosophically accepted 20 years ago, it only recently became a reality. Only in late 1985 were patrons in a few libraries able to enter a search and obtain information about materials on order, in process, on the shelf, in circulation, or at the bindery. The concept of providing holdings information through a card or microform catalog was changed to one of providing availability information.

Turnkey Vendors

The vigor of library and information-center automation development during the seventies attracted commercial vendors. The typical vendor offers a turnkey system, one that includes all hardware, software, installation, training, and ongoing support from a single source. From one vendor of turnkey or packaged systems in 1974, the market grew to accommodate nine vendors in 1979. Between 1979 and 1985, nine more vendors entered the turnkey market, but five dropped out. Nevertheless, turnkey systems accounted for more than 80 percent of local library system installations from 1975 to 1985.

The dynamic nature of the market today is primarily attributable to the availability of low cost, powerful minicomputers. The commercial vendors were able to purchase hardware, develop software packages, and market and install systems for a fraction of the cost of mainframe-based systems. In the beginning of turnkey system development, the relatively small size of the available minicomputers limited their usage to single function systems and precluded the use of such systems by large libraries and information centers; their cost precluded their use by small ones.

The capabilities of the currently available mini- and supermini-based turnkey systems are such that they can not only support the operations of large libraries, but can be configured to support systems shared by a number of large libraries. The sharing of systems has not reduced the costs of automating—as some librarians had expected—but it has facilitated resource sharing in local areas. A patron or staff member at a terminal in one location can display the resources of the libraries and information centers of an entire area. Inquiries can be directed to the holding location or the terminal operator can arrange for document delivery. Once the political problems of resource sharing are overcome, libraries and information centers can begin to plan their collection development to mesh with the collections and acquisition patterns of others.

Minicomputer technology will continue to shape the pattern of library and information-center automation development, even for smaller organizations. This is because the software packages beginning to emerge for multiuser, multitasking microcomputers are those developed for minis and transferred to smaller machines that share an architecture or design. Unlike the single-function systems built around personal micros, the multiuser systems, often designated "supermicros," can support up to 15 terminals and perform several functions concurrently.

The turnkey approach to library and information center automation will probably continue to dominate because it offers relatively low and predictable costs, a product that can usually be evaluated in an operating environment, and the clear fixing of legal responsibility for overall system performance—that is, that hardware and software work together. In contrast, most vendors of software packages do not offer the same degree of ongoing support, so the customers usually have to modify and maintain the packages they purchase. No vendor that sells only software will assume responsibility for total system performance. As compared with the distributed systems bibliographic utilities have from time to time espoused, the turnkey standalone systems offer a great degree of in-house control over local functions such as inventory control (including circulation) and patron access catalog while spreading the costs of research, development, programming, and maintenance of the automated system among many customers.

As of mid-1986 all of the turnkey systems included inventory or circulation control—in most cases extremely sophisticated packages with extensive tables of options. Virtually all systems now use barcoded labels to minimize the keying of item and patron information. The de facto standard is Codabar symbology and the CLSI "dumb label" format. Virtually all vendors can support it, thus permitting a library or information center to change computer systems without relabeling its collection.

Local cataloging capability is generally available, but not all turnkey vendors provided full MARC editing capability—a capability that permits users to create records that conform to widely adopted national standards for recording bibliographic information in machine-readable form. Acquisitions modules are available from most vendors and patron access catalogs from half of them. Most of the available patron access catalog software supports both key-word and Boolean searching. Media booking is offered by three vendors and three others have it under active development. Authority control recently has been developed in response to libraries' demands for improved data base creation and maintenance capabilities. One vendor offers word processing.

Serials control, while available from some vendors, is not expected to be available generally until late 1986. The initial offerings will provide ordering, claiming, check-in, and funds control capabilities; but routing, binding, and some of the other functions may be delayed for another six to twelve months.

Bibliographic Utilities

Shared cataloging networks such as OCLC, RLIN, WLN, and UTLAS will continue to have a major effect on the patterns of development of library automation. OCLC has revenues of more than $65 million a year, and the largest research and development staff in librarianship.

By 1986 all of the bibliographic utilities supported not only cataloging, but also acquisitions and interlibrary loans. OCLC also offered serials control and a union listing subsystem. None had moved into the area of distributed systems, although such developments have been widely forecast.

All of the utilities offer support for the retrospective conversion of manual records into machine-readable form, but only OCLC has turned it into a multimillion-dollar service. OCLC not only discounts charges for online retrospective conversion undertaken in off hours, but also contracts to perform the keying at its facilities. UTLAS realizes over 40 percent of its income from various products, including COM catalogs, acquisition lists, magnetic tapes, and catalog cards.

The development of integrated multifunction local systems has led a number of bibliographic utility participants to limit the role of their utility to that of a resource data base supplier. After obtaining a machine-readable record from a utility's data base, many participants subsequently search and edit locally. As interfaces are developed among the local library and information center systems in a region, the use of the utilities' data bases for interlibrary loan also changes. Already some participants use the utilities' interlibrary loan subsystems only to access out-of-state locations. The role of local automation is thus broadening and that of the utilities is narrowing.

Commercial Suppliers of Records

The nonprofit bibliographic utilities are being challenged by the distribution of bibliographic data by commercial firms. In the past, no commercial vendor has obtained more than $1.5 million a year in revenue from the sale of bibliographic records because none could offer a data base as rich as those of the bibliographic utilities. Some recent unpublished client studies[1] suggest that were the LC MARC tapes—the machine-readable tapes of cataloging produced by the Library of Congress—enhanced with the cataloging of a select number of libraries and information centers, a data base could be created that would meet a high percentage of the requirements of most organizations. Were a vendor to utilize the economical digital videodisc, optical digital disk, or CD-ROM disk as storage and distribution media, thus eliminating telecommunications costs, the costs of delivering the records would be substantially lower than the costs incurred by the utilities. It would not be necessary to maintain a large online data base to produce disks of machine-readable records. This would further reduce the vendor's costs. The economies of the digital videodisc and optical digital disk—in both cases plastic disks 12 to 14 inches in diameter with 1 to 4 billion characters of data encoded on the surface and read by a computer-controlled laser—are impressive. Once a master is made, videodiscs can be replicated rapidly at very low cost. While the optical digital disk can theoretically be replicated, the emphasis at this time is on the DRAW (direct-read-after-write disk), which is encoded one to six disks at a time—the latter by linking several devices. Optical digital disks can be recorded on-site and have the potential for better performance than digital videodiscs. CD-ROM disk can accommodate up to 600 million characters. CD-ROM disks are somewhat smaller disks based on compact disc technology popular in the music industry. The main advantage of this technology over videodisc and optical digital disk is that the disk drives are considerably less expensive.

It will take time for data base distributors to look beyond the videodisc's entertainment applications (which use analog signals) to the medium's capacity for storing machine-readable (digital) information. Several firms have already produced digitally encoded videodiscs and a number of others have products in development; however, only Library Systems & Services Inc. has incorporated the technology into a product, MiniMARC. The stand-alone cataloging support product contains only Library of Congress Cataloging records. GRC, however, has recently introduced a product with an enriched data base.

The Library Corporation has adopted CD-ROM as its technology and has placed cataloging bibliographic systems in 100 libraries and information centers and 50 book stores. The data base is limited to Library of Congress records.

Still, the major challenge facing the developer of a commercial bibliographic service— irrespective of the storage and distribution medium chosen—would be building a data base. Even the LC MARC tapes contain less than half the number of bibliographic records available from a utility. The utilities' requirement that participants input all of their original cataloging into the systems enables them to create the comprehensive data bases that have become their principal asset. There has been limited research undertaken to determine the minimum number of contributing libraries and information centers that would be needed to build a data base as large as that created by the 5,000 OCLC participants. It may require only a few dozen very large libraries or a well-selected combination of highly specialized libraries and information centers to provide a high hit rate for most potential customers.

By late 1986 a number of other bibliographic products are expected to become available on disks, including the types of abstracting and indexing bibliographic data bases now accessed through BRS and Dialog. The majority of the products will be offered on CD-ROM. Full-text data bases—the first of which, the Grolier Electronic Encyclopedia, was introduced in 1986, are not expected to be common except as demonstration products before late 1987 and will probably be on digitally encoded videodiscs as well as CD-ROM. One vendor has a full-text videodisc-based product in the market place—the text of the *U.S. Code* and the *Code of Federal Regulation*. No optical digital DRAW disk product is expected within the next two years.

The emphasis of electronic publishers will be on producing disks that have information stored in standard ASCII code (machine-readable character-by-character format). This form of encoding utilizes the maximum capacity of the disk and permits full-text searching. Republishers look upon the medium as a technique for storing images of pages. This is less efficient from a storage standpoint, but avoids the difficulties and costs of converting hard-copy text to ASCII. DRAW systems, which are expected to be the most popular for in-house creation of disks, are expected to be predominantly image systems for the first several years because most organizations will continue to have predominantly printed materials.

State and Regional Networks

State and regional bibliographic networks may emerge. In 1983 some concern was being expressed that state library agencies might replace their statewide COM catalogs with online data bases that could be used by local libraries and information centers not only for interlibrary loan, but also to support cataloging and retrospective conversion. It was feared that this could reduce the revenue of the utilities and possibly place these local records and thus the holding data essential for interlibrary loan, beyond the reach of libraries and information centers in other states. The concerns appear not to be justified. Information Systems Consultants Inc. surveyed all 50 state library agencies in 1983 on behalf of the Library of Congress Network Advisory Committee and determined that only one-fourth planned to support the development of statewide or regional data bases. In most cases these plans were by small states that envisioned the sharing of multifunction turnkey systems among major libraries and information centers, much as consortia in other states have done on a local level. Two states foresaw only the creation of data bases of brief records to support interlibrary lending.

To date, such state or regional networks have focused on public libraries, and in some cases, the libraries of publicly supported academic institutions. As the technologies to support linkages among separate automated library systems improves, however, there is the potential for the development of networks of libraries and information centers with special subject interests. Such a concept was the basis for automation planning among the major law libraries in the New York City area.

In only two states was there an active effort to create a statewide online data base that could be used in lieu of a bibliographic utility for online cataloging and interlibrary loan support. The low level of interest in launching a major cataloging data base is understandable because the costs are high. Consultants for the Saskatchewan Provincial Library have determined that a provincial data base limited to cataloging and interlibrary loan support would not be cost effective because there would be too few transactions against the data base in relation to the high cost of mounting and maintaining the data base and the requisite hardware and software.

A brief follow-up study in 1985 determined that the majority of the state library agencies planned to continue their COM catalogs for interlibrary loan locations, or envisioned the continued use of the ILL subsystems of the utilities, or anticipated the linkage of several of the turnkey systems in their states. The last of these options represents a rapidly emerging interest among libraries and information centers throughout North America. Some states now have so many local library systems that half or more of the state's bibliographic resources would be available online were the systems electronically linked.

Computer-to-Computer Communication

Electronic linkages or interfaces among automated library and information center systems are technically feasible, but until recently only limited progress has been made in implementing them. The 1977 study on interfaces conducted under the auspices of the National Commission on Libraries and Information Science had virtually no direct effect on the development of interfaces among local systems because it emphasized linkage across the top among the various utilities and the Library of Congress. The implementation of this approach—the Linked Systems Project—was well underway in 1986. The Linked Systems Project has led to the development of NISO (National Information Standards Organization) standards for interfacing, which could be used in local linkages.

On the local system level, the most common interface is one that involves the ability to access another computer system from a terminal on one's own system or a terminal-to-computer interface. The major drawback to this approach is that the operator of the local system has to communicate with the remote system using the language and search protocols of the remote system. While it is not unreasonable to expect a staff member to master the requirements of one or two remote systems in addition to those of the local system, there is clearly a limit to the number of systems about which any one individual can be knowledgeable. Such terminal-to-computer linkages effectively preclude direct use of the interfaces by patrons.

The greatest potential appears to lie in the open system interconnection (OSI) reference model, an international group of standards for linking heterogeneous computer systems. There are seven levels of linking standards spelled out in the model and commercially available hardware and software is generally available for the four lowest levels. Almost all of the major turnkey vendors of automated library and information center systems now support these linking standards in their hardware and software. In June 1984, UNINET, one of North America's major value added common carriers, demonstrated a linkage among several Data General-based ALIS II and one Tandem-based ALIS III library system using standards developed under the OSI reference model. While the systems came from the same vendor, they had until that time been incapable of communicating.

The type of linkage envisioned by UNINET will probably be cost effective only for interstate connections because it was designed with long distance data transmission in mind. While several regional Bell Operating Companies applied for authority to handle this type of interconnection on a local basis as early as 1983, authorization was not given until March 1985, because of the complex review involved with the deregulation of the telephone industry. By late 1986 a few pilot systems were operational. It may be 1989 before service is available throughout the United States. If these linkages become a reality, the importance of the local library systems will increase once again.

Remote Data Base Searching

The terminals of local library and information center systems will be used to search files other than the data bases of other libraries and information centers. While most organizations now have one or more separate terminals for searching remote data bases offered by the various data base services, the trend is to specify that terminals on the local automated library or information center system also be capable of accessing these remote data bases. It is highly likely that dedicated terminals will give way to universal terminals that can be used to access the local system, remote library and information center systems, a bibliographic utility, and remote data bases offered by data base services or other organizations. If such terminals are configured on personal micros, the same "workstation" can also be used to undertake office functions such as word processing and statistical analysis; and subsequently, to access disk-based data bases.

Publicly available computerized data bases numbered 1,500 as of 1985, an increase of 950 since 1979. Some 130 of these files had emerged in a six month period. Only one online service—DIALOG—offered access to more than 100 data bases, while most of the other 188 services in North America and Europe offered only one data base. Of the data bases, 980 were available through only one online service; some data bases were very popular, however, being offered by as many as 28 online services. Thirty of the online services were European; they offered more than 230 data bases, two-thirds of which could be accessed only by dialing into a European host.

There were 770 data bases that could be described as source data bases: files that provide the actual information sought, whether it be numerical, textual/numerical, or full-text. Another 630 were reference data bases: files that point to publications, people, products, or companies. One-third of the reference data bases were bibliographic and two-thirds were nonbibliographic. The rest were data bases that were not clearly source or reference types. The number of nonbibliographic data bases is increasing faster than the number of bibliographic data bases.

The most diverse online service specializing in nonbibliographic data bases is I.P. Sharp Associates of Toronto, a company that mounted its first nonbibliographic data base in 1973. Its data bases include extensive statistical data about agriculture, manufacturing, and a number of other fields. In addition to offering access to data bases through its own international telecommunications network and Telex, I.P. Sharp also offers software to manipulate the data retrieved. Sharp's best known software package, MAGIC, facilitates the merging, cumulation, analysis, formatting, and printing of data as required. Data drawn from Sharp data bases can be combined with data from other sources.

The other comprehensive online service for source data bases is Data Resources Inc. (DRI), a company owned by McGraw-Hill. It has some 55 data bases that it produces or markets under license for other firms. In addition to the data bases themselves, it offers software and consultation to facilitate the manipulation of the data. Recently, the company has begun to move toward full-text data bases. DRI's Data Pro Services, the computer hardware/software report service, is among the first of these.

While libraries and information centers will continue to offer data base searching services, it is likely that an increasing percentage of total searching activity will be undertaken by the end users or their own assistants. The experts in the library or information center, therefore, may have to provide a substantial amount of data base searching training. In addition, they may be called upon to provide conference searching—searches in which two terminals at different locations are simultaneously connected to the same data base, one of them at the end user location and the other in the library or information center. The parties see the same thing on the screen and can communicate by telephone to discuss the appropriate next step. Custom engineering to link terminals in this way is necessary because there are no conference searching packages available yet.

The Terminal Is the System

Increasing the resources available to the user of a single terminal is a major step forward, but it requires that access to the system(s) be much easier than it is now. As has been observed, patrons tend not to use an information retrieval system whenever it is more troublesome to obtain the information than not to obtain it. To most users, the terminal is the computer. Resistance to the terminal means resistance to the system.

There will, therefore, be increasing emphasis on the development of user-friendly terminals. The use of a terminal is perceived as a pleasant or unpleasant experience depending on the confidence felt by the user. The more special command language that has to be learned and the greater the chance of making a mistake, the greater the discomfort of the user and the greater the resistance to the technology. That problem will increase as libraries and information centers install more terminals for use by patrons.

There are two aspects to this problem: first, the elimination of the need for the user to know the correct method for entering a query—where the blanks belong, where the commas go, and whether periods are needed after initials; second, the ability to provide inexperienced users with a series of detailed instructions, while allowing more experienced users to bypass the instructions and get directly to the information they seek.

Turnkey automated system vendors that rely on the manufacturers of the equipment for field support are often reluctant to modify off-the-shelf terminals, but many of the improvements that might be made can be achieved by altering the appearance of the keyboard by using color-coded keys to define the various functions or displaying instructional graphics on the screen at the beginning of a procedure.

Micros as Workstations

The so-called "dumb" terminals that currently predominate on local systems are gradually being displaced by personal micros used as terminals. A micro not only offers storage and programming capability for downloading and editing search results, but it can be made more user cordial by mounting specialized search assistance programs. For example, the IBM PC may now be used to search LEXIS and NEXIS because a software package has been developed to emulate the characteristics of the dedicated terminals that were required in the past to access these systems. OCLC has developed a series of such packages to facilitate use of its various subsystems. An IBM PC with a special PROM (programmable read only memory) can function as a dedicated OCLC terminal. It offers both access to the OCLC telecommunications network and can display the full ALA character set. CLSI and Information Access Corporation jointly offer a product called Search Helper; software that can be installed on a personal micro or a mini to facilitate searching of the IAC data bases. Other companies have developed similar products.

Virtually all vendors of automated library and information center systems are moving toward the support of micro-based workstations. The IBM PC (or an IBM PC clone) is almost always the first choice. A few vendors also support the Apple II. When equipped with an ink jet printer—available for under $700—the combination is a versatile and remarkably quiet workstation. Several workstations can share a faster, more rugged printer that prints at 300 lines per minute but costs less than $3,000.

Building Local Data Bases

As staff and patrons begin to think of terminals or micros as windows to many data bases, there will be increasing interest in converting the many manual files and indexes that most libraries and information centers maintain to machine-readable form. Extracting records from a resource data base has been a cost effective way of building a local bibliographic data base, but for highly specialized files and indexes there is no counterpart to a utility or commercial bibliographic service. What is needed is a fast, low-cost method of electronically converting printed or typewritten text into machine-readable form. Despite progress in optical character recognition technology, no one has yet been able to satisfactorily scan catalog cards or similar records.

Despite several trials that have ended in failure, there is still the potential for a major breakthrough in record conversion. Kurzweil Computer Products, a subsidiary of the Xerox Corporation, manufactures the only truly omnifont optical scanner that can read a wide variety of type fonts. The Kurzweil Data Entry Machine (KDEM) is unique in that it creates a new set of digital character descriptions for each print set it scans. Conventional OCR scanners have the character descriptions for the selected font(s) installed at the factory. The Kurzweil approach gives the system great flexibility, but requires time to "train" the machine to identify the characters as they are encountered in each job. Only the basic character shapes are actually installed in the KDEM; the variations for each print set/job have to be set up with the assistance of an operator. The operator may correct the identification or confirm it, instructing the machine to continue. Corrections can be incorporated into the system's character definition tables for future use.

The speed at which the Kurzweil machine will convert printed text to machine-readable form depends on the size of the characters used in the text, the number of varieties of characters and fonts, the quality of the print, and the page format. The system can normally convert between 30 and 100 characters per second with a claimed error rate of one in 20,000 characters. Several of the machines that are now available for less than $35,000 are in use for converting printed materials into machine-readable form. The devices appear to achieve the claimed performance rates when converting legal documents, telephone directories, and other typed and printed materials that are very regular in format; but they have been unsuccessful in converting library records, reference books, and other types of materials of interest to libraries because these use proportional spacing, multiple type fonts, and diacritics—all factors that adversely affect system performance.

There are a number of limitations to the KDEM. The text must be fed to the scanner without graphics and in a single column. This means cutting out pictures and tables and folding or cutting two-column text into single columns. This requires manual preparation of the text beyond simply placing a stack of pages into the feeder. The equipment also cannot retain underlining. Another important consideration is that certain information about the printed text is lost. There is no mechanism to "remember" or record a block of space where a table or illustration appears. This type of information might be encoded within the text by the operator when reviewing the output. Another alternative might be to define certain fonts as indicators of a new section or unit of text and to develop a computer program to organize the final product.

In testing the KDEM on complex printed material such as multicolumn page formats and text in a large variety of fonts, interspersed with graphics and illustrations—the throughput rate has been disappointing. For example, the average throughput of the text of a major U.S. encyclopedia was only 27 cps. There is no doubt, however, that the machine does perform well on less complex monograph or typescriptlike materials—especially if the text has been prepared according to a set of formatting standards.

Kurzweil has recently released a new high speed system based on the MAX minicomputer. Representatives claim that the KDEM II is 200 to 500 percent faster than the KDEM I, an increase achieved through the simultaneous scanning and processing of two to five lines of text at a time. The system incorporates text processing capabilities and the ability to capture and retain underlining.

Despite the progress being made with omni-font recognition equipment, virtually 95 percent of the large-scale conversion being undertaken today involves the use of off-shore (out-of-the-country) keying service. Any program to use the Kurzweil equipment should be preceded by a pilot project using rental equipment or a service bureau. While such a pilot project should include as diverse as possible a range of documents, it should ideally involve as few people as possible to facilitate training and communication about problems. It should also be limited to 1,000 or fewer document pages a month.

In the commercial sector, an increasing percentage of publishers now have their texts in machine-readable form because they were submitted that way by the authors, because they periodically revise the same text and want the advantage of online editing, or because they use automation in typesetting. It can be expected that these firms will gradually begin to offer their publications in electronic form—probably on digitally encoded videodisc, CD-ROM, or optical digital disk. The disks could be mounted on disk drives that are hooked to a customer's minicomputer for access by multiple terminals or on personal micros for more restricted use. In addition to concerns about the technology and the economics, it will be necessary for publishers to feel protected against misuse of the information they make available in machine-readable form.

Delivery of Information to Home and Office

As patrons become accustomed to using terminals in libraries and information centers to meet their information needs they will begin to expect that they can access the same information from their offices and homes. Some libraries and information centers are already setting aside ports on their computers to facilitate dial-up access from office or home. The primary demand appears to be from the office. Despite the glowing predictions made for the sale of small home computers, only a minority of homes are expected to have computers by the end of the century.

Local Area Networks

The primary form of electronic dissemination of information to offices within an organization is expected to be through a Local Area Network (LAN). A LAN has two characteristics: it is a high-capacity telecommunications channel and it provides protocols that permit incompatible devices to communicate with one another. A LAN may support the OSI reference model. It does not utilize the telecommunications channels provided by a common carrier or public communications service. Thus, by definition, a LAN does not utilize a public telephone system, a public access long distance network, or other public means of communication. The most popular transmission media are coaxial and fiber optic cables. Each has the capacity to accommodate not only a high volume of data transfer, but also voice and video. The protocols that permit incompatible devices to connect to the network may be located in a central network processor or in a number of network interface units distributed throughout the network.

LANs have many different applications. In an office situation, a LAN can readily replace much of the paper flow with electronic documents. In this situation, the LAN can transmit the budget material generated by micro-based spreadsheets among the personal computers themselves and on to the host computer. Computer resources can be shared building or campus-wide, with each terminal or micro being able to access every computer. High-speed printers, plotters, CAD (computer aided design) units, and other special devices can be shared among many users. Data bases can be made available throughout the building or campus.

A LAN is normally limited to 25 kilometers. It may, therefore, be used to connect several buildings on a campus, but it is not suitable for connecting buildings at some distance from one another. There must, therefore, be an interface between the LAN and the networks that span larger areas. Special software permits devices on a LAN to be connected by "gateways" through their CPUs to external data services or long distance communication systems.

LANs are still in their infancy. Many of those that are offered for sale permit the connection of many kinds of devices, but do not offer true interconnectivity. The incompatible devices share the channel and stay out of one another's way, but the protocols that permit true linkage are still under development.

While LANs are quite new, some 16,000 have been installed, about two-thirds of them in office environments. Equally important as a measure of the penetration of the technology is the number of LAN-connected devices—machines currently linked by a LAN. As of 1984 that figure was in excess of 125,000; and by 1989 the figure is expected to exceed 1 million. Also important to the future of LANs is the total market value; projections estimate a total of $850 million in 1986 and a total of over $3 billion by 1989.

Brown University in Providence, Rhode Island, installed one of the first large multibuilding LANs. The Brown system, designated BRUNET, will ultimately link 110 buildings and provide more than 1,000 connections. The long-term goal is to connect BRUNET to all offices, lecture rooms, laboratories, and dorms. The host devices connected via BRUNET include DEC VAX 11–780s, IBM 4341s, and IBM 370–158/3 processors. The network provides concurrent 9600 bit/second connections for hundreds of ASCII terminals. In addition, it supports dial-in services for nonconnected users and includes a gateway connection for access to external services. BRUNET also handles a campus-wide energy management system, a campus security system, and closed circuit television transmission.

Installation of BRUNET began in 1981. The cost of the primary, or backbone, LAN distribution system was $317,000. The total cost of additional items such as service equipment, 1,600 building wiring outlets, and other items, was an additional $1.024 million.

An examination of 20 LANs has established that the hardware cost if from $400 to $1,000 per node to physically link devices and the development of the software for the higher levels of the linkages can cost tens of thousands of dollars—the biggest constraint on the use of LANs today is the fact that software development for the linkages is still very incomplete. The most common approach today is to put an organization's major computers and a large number of personal micros on the network and to move information from one mini or mainframe to another by passing it through the micros and reformatting it. This involves only an investment in commercially available micro-mini and/or micro-mainframe downloading and uploading packages.

Videotex Systems

The technology that is most widely promoted for distribution of data to homes and of offices is "Videotex." The term videotex is generally used as the generic name for information retrieval via a modified home television set and, in some cases, is interpreted to applying to any dialog between a host computer and a home or office micro. In more precise usage, it refers to those systems in which the information is distributed over telephone lines or cable. In this sense videotex is different from teletext in which information is broadcast to the home using the black space between the frames (the vertical blanking interval) of regular broadcast television images. Because they rely on wiring to deliver information, true videotex systems can operate in a two-way or interactive mode, allowing the user not only to receive information, but also to transmit data back to the system. A mainframe or minicomputer is used at the "head end" of the system so that many users can be served at one time. The decoder attached to the television receiver can accept data at a faster rate than a conventional television set and can also be used to formulate control signals to be sent back to the host computer.

Videotex systems can display diagrams and text in any of several sizes and in color. Once the text is displayed it can be read like a book, and the viewer can page through the screens of data. In contrast with teletext where the number of frames handled by the system is limited by the broadcast medium— effectively to the length of time a user is prepared to wait until the desired frame is broadcast sequentially—videotex can provide users with access to hundreds of thousands of pages of data.

In both videotex and teletext systems, the first thing the user sees is a contents page or menu, which provides a rundown on the information available and directs the user to the subindexes for the various sections. From the subindex the user is directed to specific pages of information. The modified television set has a small remote-control keypad (similar to that of a hand-held calculator) for controlling the system. In interactive videotex systems that keypad can also be used to place orders, perform calculations, or send other types of messages.

There were more than 100 trials of videotex and teletext systems underway in the U.S. in 1986 and some announcements of operational systems had been made. Several news media had contracted to provide news, and several retailers were planning to use videotex systems for advertising, with online ordering available to the viewer. The weather, stock market reports, and sports results were among other information available. The information may be priced on the basis of the number of pages displayed or as part of a monthly subscription.

In Britain—where the systems are fully operational—the charges paid by the suppliers of information range from $2.50 to $8 per page annually on top of a minimum charge of $2,000 to $8,000, depending on the type of service offered.

There will obviously be copyright considerations in any such electronic use of published information by libraries and information centers. A publisher might insist that only it could legitimately distribute electronically what it has produced. Licensing or royalty payment agreements would probably have to be negotiated. For that reason, the most likely data bases for libraries and information centers to deliver initially would be their own catalogs and local files.

Not all commentators are sanguine about the long-term future of videotex, despite the fact that the technology represents a breakthrough in information retrieval and transaction processing. Several studies have concluded that videotex is simply too unsophisticated for most business applications. In 1986 two operational systems were discontinued. Nevertheless, AT&T and IBM have both recently increased their investments in the technology. Their mere presence in the market increases the long-term viability of videotex. The trend may be toward integrated data processing/videotex/management computing systems, rather than toward videotex as an isolated medium. Several terminals that can display both videotex and computing formats are already being marketed.

Data Communications Costs as a Factor in Technology Use

Increased use of automation and other technologies has been encouraged by the rapid reductions in costs over the past decade. The implication of the trends we have been examining is that they will require much greater use of data communications facilities: the one area in which costs have been rising, especially locally. Libraries and information centers have, therefore, been examining a number of alternatives to the use of telephone lines, among them satellites, microwave, coaxial cable, and fiber optics.

The prospects are not bright in the foreseeable future. Satellites are economically viable only for long distance links—distances greater than 500 miles. Microwave—a technology that is normally deemed cost effective for distances of 25 to 500 miles requires substantial outlays for the sending and receiving equipment. Coaxial cable and fiber optics—both potentially cost effective at distances from 1,000 feet and up—can be implemented in a local area network without a license, but linking different parts of a community or a state requires licensing as a common carrier.

No single technology can be used to meet all of a library or information center's data communications needs. The scale required for cost effective use of any technology precludes any adoption independent of the parent organization. Even a large organization may find it necessary to continue to purchase most of the telecommunications services it needs from a local telephone company, special common carrier such as MCI, or a local cable TV company.

The major impact of telecommunications technology on libraries and information technologies would appear to be the use of telecommunications hardware such as modems and multiplexors, rather than the adoption of complex new devices.

Moving Hard Copy

It may take several more years before a substantial percentage of the information libraries and information centers seek to collect is in machine-readable form. A scenario more plausible than a paperless, disembodied library or information center is one with a combination of hard-copy and electronic information. A library or information center's collection typically grows at a rate of 5 percent per year. Were an organization to commit half of its acquisitions budget to information in electronic form, it would still have some three-quarters of its collection in hard copy after two decades. It appears quite likely that at least for the next 20 years libraries will have to be designed with room for books, journals, and readers at tables. But they will also have to accommodate computer rooms, computer terminals, and a number of other electronic devices.

Because of the continued existence of hard-copy information, it will be necessary for libraries to implement systems to electronically transfer information not in machine-readable form. A number of libraries already are using digital telefacsimile for this purpose. The technology is discussed in Chapter 6.

Automating Office Procedures

When automation was introduced into libraries and information centers, it was applied to clerical and repetitive tasks. With the growing emphasis on improving the inquiry features of circulation systems and supporting the online searching of bibliographic data bases, traditional office procedures have been overlooked. Many organizations have already realized considerable improvements in office productivity by installing word processing equipment to speed typing and text editing. There are many other office operations that readily lend themselves to automation. Among them are storage and retention of correspondence and unpublished reports, coordination of meetings, relaying of messages, preparation of budgets, and analysis of statistical data. While an integrated information system could be used for these tasks in addition to unique library/information center tasks, the best and least expensive software packages for all of these applications are written for micros.

Ideally the office micro(s) would be able to function as terminals to the library/information center system and records could be passed back and forth between the two systems.

The automation of the office will be relatively inexpensive compared with the automation of other parts of the library or information center because development costs can be shared among tens of thousands of organizations of all types which use the same software.

Summary and Outlook

By 1995, the majority of the libraries and information centers of North America will be automated. The libraries and information centers will not be paperless, however. Acquisitions decisions will be based on extensive management information about patrons and patterns of collection use, ordering will be online, and funds accounting will be done automatically. Shared cataloging will be a by-product of shared bibliographic data bases mounted on bibliographic utility systems or distributed on videodisc or CD-ROM disk.

Online patron access catalog and inventory or circulation control functions will be commonplace because they have the greatest potential value for patrons. The patron will be able to access both the holdings and current availability status of materials locally and in other libraries and information centers with which the system is linked. The patron will also be able to access the system from a terminal in any location within the facility or from the home or office using a terminal, micro, or a television receiver adapted for videotex.

Many of the terminals in the library or information center will be micro-based workstations that can access not only the library or information center data base, but many other local and remote data bases. Linkages to other systems will probably be through the micro-based workstations. Software in the micro will facilitate the manipulation and reformatting of the information. Automation will also have extended to the library/information center office.

Libraries and information centers will continue to have collections of printed materials, but a significant percentage of the core reference collection will be accessed through computer terminals. Statistical, directory, and bibliographic information will become available in machine-readable form by the late 1980s. The electronic publications that need to be revised only a few times a year will probably be distributed on digitally encoded videodisc or CD-ROM, with replacements sent by mail. The publications that need to be updated regularly will be distributed on optical digital disks that can be revised by downloading information from a remote resource data base or by loading floppy disks provided by the supplier.

Back files of journals, patents, and other types of materials now often maintained on microform will be stored on optical media for faster retrieval—both within the library/information center and remotely from elsewhere in the organization.

The library/information center will provide information

to remote users by local area network and possible through videotex systems to homes.

The implications of this scenario for the planning of library and information center facilities is the subject of this book. Each of the technologies that are expected to have a significant impact on space requirements in the next decade is described in the following chapters.

Note

1. Information Systems Consultants Inc. studies for a bibliographic service company, 1986.

3

AUTOMATED LIBRARY SYSTEMS

In Chapter 2, library automation was identified as the single most significant information technology. Because of the large number of books and articles on library automation, and because most librarians are now quite conversant with this technology, this chapter will not discuss the technology in detail. The discussion will be limited to the major facilities planning implications. Addressed are space, electrical and telecommunications, environmental, and layout issues.

Space Requirements

A library or information center that has or envisions a local, multifunction, integrated library system will require an electronic equipment room large enough to accommodate a computer, a console with printer, one or more disk drives, one line printer, one magnetic tape drive, and one telecommunications rack. These are the minimum requirements regardless of the size of the library or the system. The space requirements will vary depending not only on the size of the system, but also on the manufacturer of the equipment selected. The electrical and air conditioning requirements will vary even more than space requirements.

The space and other requirements set forth in this chapter are based on a mid-size minicomputer supporting 30 to 60 terminals, the most common type of system sold in the period 1980–85. A supermicro supporting 6 to 30 terminals will normally require two-thirds as much space, a supermini supporting 60 to 120 terminals up to twice as much, and a mainframe or cluster of superminis potentially several times as much.

Because of the complexity of an automated library system and because of the many variations in requirements, the exact placement of a system's components must be worked out with the vendor's field service personnel. The amount of space required by the mini equipment itself will be up to 180 square feet if it is installed per manufacturers' specifications. Staff and storage space would require an additional 50 square feet. The total requirement can be reduced from 230 to 200 square feet if the CPU and disk drives are placed side by side without the prescribed air space. This would increase the air conditioning requirements, however.

The space requirements can be separated into central site, storage, and remote peripheral space.

CENTRAL SITE HARDWARE

The following section represents typical equipment dimensions, and is based upon Digital Equipment Corporation, Data General, and Microdata hardware, with dimensions rounded upward.

Processor:

Width:	2'
Height:	3'6"
Depth:	2'6"
Weight:	450 lbs.

Consoles (including stand):

Width:	2'2"
Height:	3'2"
Depth:	3'
Weight:	700 lbs.

Disk Drives (each, 300 MB size):

Width:	2'
Height:	3'
Depth:	3'
Weight:	300 lbs.

Printer:

Width:	2'9"
Height:	3'9"
Depth:	2'2"
Weight:	370 lbs.

Magnetic Tape Drive:

Width:	1'10"
Height:	3'6"
Depth:	2'6"

Modems/Multiplexors (8 units/rack-mounted):

Width:	1'10"
Height:	5'6"
Depth:	1'8"

Uninterruptable Power Supply (UPS): An UPS continues to deliver power after a power failure. They are not normallly used with library systems, but if one is planned, a space 3 feet wide and 2 feet deep against a wall will be needed.

Free Space

For each piece of equipment, free space should be available to allow for air flow.

Front of unit:	5' free space
Rear of unit:	4' free space

Units except for printers may be placed such that they abut other systems components (i.e., no free space at the sides), as long as specified free space is provided at the front and rear. This will increase the air conditioning requirement by as much as 40 percent.

STORAGE SPACE

There are considerable storage requirements associated with an automated system:

Disk Packs

Some vendors use disk drives with removable disk packs. For each data base disk drive there are usually five disks: one "run" disk, and four backup disks. There are usually two additional disks for use by the vendor's service personnel.

The run disks are housed in the disk drives during normal operations. One set of backup disks must be stored in a remote location separate from the building to safeguard the data base in the event of a disaster. The other three sets of backup disks may be stored in the computer room.

The disks must be stored flat side down and may not be stacked. The disks must be stored in a dust-free environment. Disk storage cabinets may be made to order or may be purchased from a data processing supply vendor. Tightly constructed standard metal cabinets with adjustable shelves may also be used.

Disk pack dimensions (each, 300MB size):

Diameter:	1'3"
Depth:	7"
Weight:	20 lbs.

Paper Supplies Paper, ribbons, and other supplies must be stored outside, but near the computer room. Two regular metal supply cabinets should accommodate one year's supplies.

Shipping Cartons A limited number of the cartons in which the system was shipped should be retained in case it is necessary to reship any of the components for repair or replacement. The cartons must be stored outside of the computer room.

1 carton	2'6"	× 3'6"	× 4'2"	for a processor
1 carton	1'11"	× 1'2"	× 2'3"	for a console
1 carton	2'	× 1'	× 2'4"	for a console stand
1 carton	3'4"	× 2'2"	× 3'9"	for a disk drive
1 carton	1'9"	× 1'9"	× 11"	for a disk
1 carton	3'	× 2'3"	× 5'	for a printer
1 carton	2'6"	× 1'9"	× 11"	for tape drive component
1 carton	2'6"	× 2'	× 2'8"	for tape drive component
1 carton	2'6"	× 1'10"	× 5'	for tape drive component
3 cartons	2'4"	× 1'10"	× 1'6"	for multiplexors
3 cartons	1'6"	× 1'1"	× 8"	for terminals

Documentation
    4 3" binders containing user instructions
    6 3" binders for hardware documentation for use by
vendor field service personnel

REMOTE PERIPHERALS

Remote peripherals include terminals, micro-based workstations, and side printers. A micro-based workstation is a personal computer with storage being used as both a terminal and
a standalone processor. A side printer is a printer used to print
directly from the screen of a terminal or micro-based workstation. Side printers are usually attached to only a small number
of circulation and patron access catalog terminals, but almost
always to micro-based workstations. The number of devices is
typically determined by a formula such as the following:

- 1 circulation terminal for each 70,000 circulations per year
  or significant fraction thereof at a service point;
- 1 patron access catalog terminal/workstation per 100 patrons entering the library or information center in the
  course of a day;
- 1 staff inquiry terminal/workstation for each reference
  point;
- 1 acquisitions terminal/workstation for each 10,000 titles
  ordered in a year;
- 1 serials control terminal/workstation for each 50,000 issues received in a year; and
- 1 data base editing terminal/workstation for each 10,000
  records added to the data base each year.

    While the typical terminal is 1'4" in width and 1'8" in
depth, each terminal will require a surface no smaller than 3
feet wide and 2 feet deep (6 square feet) so that there will be
ample workspace and air movement around the device. The
requirements are the same for micro-based workstations as for
terminals except that more space is required for a disk drive,
whether magnetic or optical. The device is typically 1 foot wide,
1 foot deep, and 8 inches high. A micro-based workstation will,
therefore, require a space 4 feet wide and 2 feet deep.

The patron access catalog terminals may be on either standing height or sitting height tables. In either case, there should be ample circulating space—at least 25–30 square feet is recommended. Carrells (the 48-inch-wide type) are ideal furniture for patron access catalog terminals/workstations. The majority of the patron access catalog terminals should be located near the major reference point where the traditional card catalog would normally be located. The remainder can be placed elsewhere in the library or information center.

The implementation of a patron access catalog should not affect the location of reference and circulation points. The main reference point should continue to be located inside the entrance to the library or information center; ideally just inside the door on the right. If there is a separate circulation point, it should continue to be located opposite the main reference point. With proper graphics the traffic flow will be obvious to users: enter on the right and get assistance in using the facility, and exit on the left and charge materials on the way out. Secondary reference and/or circulation points should be similarly positioned near the entries to designated areas throughout the library or information center.

Electrical/Telecommunications Requirements

Electrical and telecommunications requirements are treated together because a single contractor is often retained for the installation of both. Each is addressed both with regard to the central site and the remote peripherals.

CENTRAL SITE

The central site requirements will vary a great deal from vendor to vendor. It is, therefore, desirable to defer electrical work until the vendor is identified. If it is necessary to construct the space without knowing the vendor, the requirements that are common to most mini-based systems are:

Power Lines

Processor: One single phase, 3-wire, dedicated line with isolated ground, 60 HZ, 20 AMP, 12 gauge, 120 volt (+6, −10). The power line must end no further than 10 feet (300 cm) from the center rear of the processor. Extension cords are not allowed. The vendor normally provides one −NEMA 5 −20R receptacle (Hubbell IG5362 or equivalent).

Console: A console is normally placed within 7 feet of its processor and is plugged into the unit, drawing its power from the processor. It does not require a separate power line.

Disk Drives (each): One single phase, 3-wire, dedicated line with isolated ground, 60 HZ, 20 AMP, 10 gauge, 208 volt (+14.6, −29). One −NEMA L6 −20R receptacle (Hubbell 2320 or equivalent). The power line must end no further than 7 feet from the rear of the drive. Extension cords are not allowed.

Tape Drive: One single-phase, 3-wire, dedicated line with isolated ground, 60 HZ, 20 AMP, 12 gauge, 120 volt (+6, −10). One −NEMA 5 −20R receptacle (Hubbell IG5362 or equivalent). The magnetic tape unit's power cord is 7 feet (210 cm) long. Extension cords may be used, but must be authorized by the vendor.

Printer: One single-phase, 3−wire, dedicated line with isolated ground, 60 HZ, 20 AMP, 12 gauge, 120 volt (+6, −10). One −NEMA 5 −20R receptacle (Hubbell IG5262 or equivalent). The printer's power cord is 10 feet long. Extension cords may be used, but must be authorized by the vendor.

Subpanel Box Some jurisdictions require a subpanel box located in the computer room for emergency power shut-off. Consult local authorities for the regulations in your area.

Line Conditioner If the library experiences high electrical "noise" and line transience, power line conditioning may be required to maintain constant line voltage with low "noise" and high transience. The most important units to protect are the disk drives. Each 300 MB drive requires a line conditioner rated at 15 KVA. Many units can be wall mounted.

Uninterruptable Power Supply (UPS)   An UPS continues to deliver power after a power failure. They are not normally used with library systems, but if one is planned, it must be carefully sized to the power requirements of the system.

Line Labels   Tag each AC power receptacle using electrical wire numbering tape to identify the subpanel box and the circuit breaker which controls it.

REMOTE PERIPHERALS

A terminal or micro-based workstation may be either hardwired to the system or connected through telephone lines or another telecommunications medium. A hardwired terminal or workstation is usually located less than 750 feet from the control room and communicates with the system via data cables that the vendor specifies, but that the library is usually responsible for having installed.

Requirements vary with the type of terminal chosen. This description, therefore, is a composite of the most common terminal choices: Digital, Data General, and Wyse.

Electrical Requirements

One single-phase, 3-wires dedicated line with isolated ground, 60 HZ, 20 AMP, 12 gauge, 120 volt ($+6$, -10) for every four terminals/workstations.

One -NEMA 5 -20R receptacle (Hubbell IG5252 or equivalent) for every terminal/workstation. The terminal/workstation's power cord is usually 4 feet long. Extension cords may be used, but must be authorized by the vendor.

Data Cables   A library or information center is usually responsible for supplying and installing the data cable between the computer room and the terminals/workstations. It is normally 4-conductor, shielded cable—Belden

8723 or equivalent. For hard-wired terminals, the length of the cable should be the distance between the system and the terminal/workstation, and an additional 7 feet at each end. For other terminals/workstations, the length of the cable should be the distance between the terminal/workstation and the telephone jack, plus an additional 7 feet at each end. Splices and multiconnector hookups are not permitted, nor can the data cable be pulled through the same conduit as the electrical wiring. The vendor provides and installs the hooded connectors at each end of the cable for hookup.

Telephone Lines   Install a voice grade, 2-wire, half-duplex, Series 3002 line for each terminal/workstation unless multiplexors are used. Multiplexors require one line each; a 4-wire, dedicated line, Series 3002, full-duplex line. It is important to note that some terminals/workstations also require a voice-grade 4–wire, full-duplex line. Lines should, therefore, not be installed until the vendor selection has been made.

For each telephone line, have the telephone company install demarcation blocks (type 42A) at the end of the telephone line, no more than 7 feet from the system and from the remote terminal. The telephone company must label both the transmit wire and the receiver wire at the demarcation blocks.

Electrical Requirements   One single-phase, 3–wire, dedicated line with isolated ground, 60 HZ, 20 AMP, 12 gauge, 120 volt (+ 6, − 10).

Telephone Requirements for Voice Communication   Install a voice-grade, nondedicated, direct line telephone with a long cord adjacent to the console of a data base processor. Consult with the local telephone company for the types of equipment that are available for a high noise area.

Telephone Power   The installation of new telephone lines frequently requires electrical considerations. Consult with the local phone company to ensure meeting its requirements.

Environmental Requirements

The following environmental conditions must be maintained for most systems:

Humidity: 40% to 60% noncondensing. Rate of change must not exceed 2% per hour.

Temperature: 65 to 75 degrees F (18 to 21 degrees C). Variance in temperature must not exceed 3.6 degrees F (2 degrees C) per hour.

BTU Output: Processor—2,500 BTUs per hour.
300 MB Drive—4,200 BTUs per hour.
Console—823 BTUs per hour.
Printer—2,335 BTUs per hour.
Mag Tape Unit—1,092 BTUs per hour.
Per Person—300 BTUs per hour.

Air Flow: The air flow rate for a system depends on a combination of specific equipment and room size. It is, therefore, necessary to oversize the air handling system when the exact combination of equipment and room is not known in advance. *If equipment is placed side by side without the recommended air space between units, BTU output for each piece of equipment should be increased 50%.*

The air conditioning system must provide filtering to reduce dust and other particle matter as much as possible. If salt air, corrosive gases, or other air pollutants are present, special filtering arrangements may be required and an air conditioning consultant should be contacted.

If the system is to be operated unattended for more than a few minutes at a time, the installation of automatic high-temperature power shutoff controls and/or remote high-temperature alarms should be provided in an attended location to forestall damage to the computer system in the event of air conditioning failure.

It may be desirable to arrange the air conditioning system so that it can provide ventilating air (though not necessarily cooled air) in emergency circumstances to facilitate fire fighting.

Consult with local fire protection authorities for advice. The air conditioning system should be provided with a central shutoff switch to facilitate emergency system shutdown.

For efficient cooling, a minimum clearance of 30 inches above the top of equipment cabinets is recommended.

PROTECTION AGAINST STATIC CONDITIONS

If the proposed site is prone to static conditions, the following is a list of precautions that may be taken to reduce the problem.

- Maintain proper humidity.
- Place each major component of the system on a non-porous, antistatic mat. Do not place the system on a carpet.
- Do not use floor wax, if the equipment is placed on a tile floor.
- Use only wooden chairs.

FIRE PROTECTION REQUIREMENTS

Typical library minicomputer installations have not included fire protection beyond hand-controlled Halon fire extinguishers. If a library wishes to install a Halon fire protection system in recognition of the sensitivity of its data and the likelihood of unattended overnight system operation, the Halon system should provide a warning tone and a time delay before the chemical is released, such that staff may operate a manual system override in case the system is accidentally activated.

Layout

Ideally the computer room will be twice as long as it is wide and the equipment will be arranged so that it can be operated from the front and serviced from the back. From the doorway at one end the machines are usually arranged in frequency of use: Console, printer, CPU, disk drives, and tape drive. The modem rack should be on the wall behind the CPU and should have a telephone outlet as well as an electrical outlet. The electrical power should be provided from the wall behind the machines. There should be a wall telephone with a long cord on the wall opposite the console (Fig. 3.1; the illustration is not to scale).

These site preparation requirements are generic. Each vendor will have specific requirements for the installation of its equipment. The generic specifications should be used only in planning new facilities or undertaking a major remodeling before a system has been selected. The specific requirements of a vendor should be used whenever the system has already been selected.

If at all possible, a library or information center should provide an extra 50 square feet in the control room for the future addition of optical storage media and a small processor to control them. This technology is discussed in detail in Chapter 5.

4
MICROFORM

Microform has been used in libraries and information centers for over 50 years and continues to be the most widely used space conserving technology. A reel of microfilm or a packet of fiche occupies up to 97 percent less space than a bound volume. Less popular microform include microprint, microcard, ultrafiche, and microaperture.

A decision to use microform is more complex than just a matter of space requirements, however, because there is labor cost involved in the selection and servicing of the microform; special reading and printing equipment must be purchased; and the users must be made comfortable with a medium different from print.

Not all microform purchases are motivated by a desire to conserve space, however. Often materials are available only on microform or the microform versions are considerably less expensive than hard copy.

Republishing characterized the microform publishing industry until the 1970s. In the period of most rapid growth of microform publishing—the 1950s and 1960s—the demands of scholars were growing dramatically, especially in the younger universities. Acquisitions budgets were also increasing rapidly, but rare and scarce materials were not always available in the original format. Some titles were available as hard-copy reprints, but many others were offered only in microform reprinted editions because the potential sales were too low to justify the printed format. Unlike hard-copy reprinting, which was then cost effective in quantities of 50 copies or more, microform republishing was practical when sales of only one to a few dozen sets could be projected. Relatively young libraries were thus able to build distinguished collections in less than two decades and mature libraries were able to preserve their collections by backing up their fragile hard-copy holdings with microform.

By the mid-1970s as sales started to level off, microform publishers began emphasizing the economics of microforms as a replacement for existing holdings, expecially for journals. The sales literature of the largest microform publisher, University Microfilms International, in 1979 characterized microform as "a system that keeps a growing library or information center from outgrowing its walls."

Librarians and information scientists are apparently not convinced that microform is the answer to their space problems. In a 1980 telephone survey of medium and large academic and public libraries, Information Systems Consultants Inc. asked library directors and microform librarians why their institutions purchased microforms. Only a small minority answered that the space-saving potential of microform was the principal justification for committing a significant percentage of acquisitions funds to the medium. Despite the changing emphasis in the promotional materials of microform publishers, collection development continues to be more significant than space-saving for librarians. There has been a shift, however, from acquiring large collections of thousands of rare and scarce monographs and journals on microfilm to the purchase of small, highly focused subject collections. Microform was chosen when hard copy was not available, when the microform cost substantially less than the hard copy, or when the purchase of microform was less expensive than binding.

Conversion Study Results

The apparent lack of interest by libraries in the space-saving potential of microforms led a major microform publisher to commission two consulting firms to develop detailed statistical data on the benefits of converting serials from hard-copy to microform. The study confirmed the industry's view that purchasing microform in lieu of binding journals is cost effective, but raised serious doubt that the retrospective conversion of a library or information center's existing hard-copy backfiles is cost effective even though significant space reductions can be realized.

The cost components associated with conversion to microform are:

1. Selection
2. Acquisition procedures
3. Cost of materials
4. Cataloging
5. Binding
6. Replacement rate
7. Weeding
8. Space
9. Storage
10. Reading facilities
11. Copying facilities
12. Equipment maintenance
13. Home circulation
14. Personnel
15. Interlibrary loan
16. Copyright
17. Administrative overhead

Tentative figures for each of these cost categories were obtained by checking the professional literatures of librarianship and micrographics. The categories and cost data were then checked by site visits to nine libraries of various sizes and types. No additions were made to the list of categories as a result of the site visits, but over 35 percent of the costs were modified on the basis of the data obtained from the libraries. The cost categories of sufficient significance to warrant their inclusion in a comparison of hard copy and microform were:

a. Selection
b. Acquisition
c. Purchase cost of materials
d. Cataloging
e. Binding
f. Replacement
g. Storage equipment
h. Space (construction and maintenance)
i. Interlibrary lending

j. Reading/printing equipment
k. Equipment maintenance

Two important figures that emerged from the site visits were the percentage of a library's holdings that are bound serials and the percentage of serial titles a library might reasonably expect to convert to microform. In all of the libraries the bound serial collections represented just under 20 percent of the volumes. The libraries could convert only a minority of these titles to microform even though microform publishers' catalogs list over 10,000 available serial titles. This is because the copyright holders of many of the titles to which libraries subscribe will not grant licenses for the reformatting of their publications to microform. For large research libraries only 12 percent of the serial holdings were actually available in microform, and for medium-sized libraries the average was approximately 32 percent. These figures are not expected to increase rapidly in the future. The figure for special libraries and information centers is approximately 25 percent.

The one-time costs of conversion to microform were determined by adding the costs of selection and acquisition, the cataloging of the converted title, storage equipment (the equipment with greatest storage capacity suitable for patron access), and the costs of acquiring and installing microform readers and printers, etc. The recurring annual costs were also determined, among them the costs of annual subscription, check-in, binding, replacement of damaged publications, storage equipment additions, amortization and maintenance of space, processing of interlibrary loans, and maintenance of microform equipment. The total five-year cost was then determined for each institution, both for the substitution of microform for binding and for retroactive conversion of bound serial volumes. The average annual savings were also determined.

Payback Period for Conversion

The payback period for purchasing microform in lieu of binding was an average of 1.5 years for research libraries and 1.3 years for libraries of other types and sizes. In other words, it would take 1.3 to 1.5 years before the recurring annual savings would compensate for the one-time cost of the substitution. The payback period averaged 14 years for all types of institutions for a retrospective conversion of bound materials. The space savings, however, would be considerable and the library could expect a drop in the rate of loss of materials.

Reducing Resistance to Microform

While there is a great deal of enthusiasm about most information technologies, it is generally held that patrons are resistant to microform. If so, there appears to be considerable opportunity for libraries to reduce resistance to microform by planning facilities and equipment selection carefully. Not only will that improve the actual experience of the microform user, but it will also change the message given to microform users: that "microforms are a last resort." This is the message when microform facilities are less attractive than the rest of the library or information center, when they are poorly arranged, or equipment is difficult to use.

Donald C. Holmes interviewed nearly 90 librarians and microform users in an Association of Research Libraries study in 1968. He wrote in his report:

The reasons given by the interviewees for using microforms were conventional, such as: material not otherwise available, to avoid keeping magazines and other serials in bound form, to preserve deteriorating material, to store bulky materials, and to provide print-out in hard-copy form in lieu of use of rare or expensive originals. . . . The lack of an optimum physical environment for microform use—suitable lighting, humidity control, suitable furniture, etc.—was deplored [by the users].[1]

Francis Spreitzer of the University of Southern California visited more than three dozen libraries of all types with a grant from the Council on Library Resources. He wrote of the facilities he saw:

The problem with microforms in libraries appears to result from neither inadequate equipment or user less resistance. It stems from general ignorance of applied micrographics.[2]

Spreitzer characterized as good less than 10 percent of the microform facilities he saw on his extensive travels.

While libraries plan the implementation of complex technologies such as automated systems very carefully, they appear to be somewhat casual about a technology as old and seemingly simple as microform. There is good reason to believe that most of the resistance of patrons to the medium has been attributable to poor facilities and equipment. Any program for systematic acquisition of microform should be adopted only after microform facilities have been carefully reviewed and any necessary improvements made. This is particularly critical if microform is selected in lieu of binding because such a program normally affects more patrons than a retrospective conversion of backfiles of serials.

Changing Usage Patterns

Before discussing proper space planning for microform, it is necessary to look at how microform use is changing. One of the reasons why microform has not more fully displaced hardcopy in libraries and information centers is that one of its chief advantages, space saving, does not benefit the actual user of the information. There is no reason for patrons to urge that microform be made available. New combinations of technologies—which bring computers, micrographics and telecommunication together—are beginning to change that. The most common generic name for such combinations of technology is Computer Assisted Retrieval (CAR).

Integrating these technologies is more cost effective than relying solely on computing because micrographics supplies the lowest cost mass memory (1/30th the cost of online disk memory), the computer provides prompt access by any one of several search terms, and telecommunications avoids the duplication of the information at several locations.

In the typical CAR system, microfilm or microfiche are stored randomly in cartridges or carousels to eliminate the possibility of misfiling. The film or fiche is indexed by author, title, subject, and other suitable access points. Index numbers are coded directly on the film or fiche, or on a carrier that holds the fiche. With computer control over the storage devices, a user can search the files from any one of a number of reading stations, retrieve a microform and see a video image of it in less than five seconds on the same terminal that has been used to access the computer. The capacities of the largest devices currently available from companies such as Access, Infodetics, Ragen, Teknekron, and Kodak is from 18 to 30 million pages per system.

The more sophisticated systems retrieve fiche from one of several carousels, digitize it (reformatting the analog information to digital form for transmission using special scanning equipment), and electronically transfer the information to a computer disk. The disk acts as a temporary storage for that image and thousands of others, allowing other users access to the carousel. The image is transferred from the disk to the video display unit which has up to 1,500 line resolution, far better than a television receiver. The image can be converted to paper using an associated "hard-copy unit" or printer. Copies cost less than $.05 per page.

Remote communication can be achieved by using existing telephone lines, cable transmission, or satellite links. The use of one of these telecommunications technologies results in simultaneous access for those at a location removed from the central files and those at the site of the central files. One of the historic problems of sharing information has been that location has affected access. Those at remote locations have had to wait for days for information to be delivered by mail or courier. The historic resistance of librarians and information scientists to shared central storage facilities has been attributed to a "not owned here" syndrome, but the author's experience is that librarians and information scientists respond positively to using remote information when immediate access is available. The extensive use of remote bibliographic data bases offered by BRS and Dialog is proof of that.

Turnkey CAR systems start at $15,000 for a desktop system. A more typical price for a system that serves a special library or information center is $95,000. Such a system could store up to two million pages. The system consists of a microfilm storage device, a micro image retrieval system, three to eight terminals, a small computer, and software. The system not only facilitates retrieval, but can be used for data entry about the documents.

Space Requirements

Microform facilities are usually quite small when compared with the buildings or rooms in which they are housed. That is reasonable, of course, because the microform format represents up to a 97 percent space saving as compared with the original hard copy. Even with the addition of up to 35 square feet for each reading position, few microform areas in large libraries exceed 5,000 square feet.

The exact requirements will depend on the types of microform and the storage equipment selected. A good rule of thumb is to estimate 100 reels of 35mm film per square foot (or 200 reels of 16mm) and 2,300 fiche per square foot if the most efficient form of cabinet storage is used: an 11-drawer unit. Microfilm reader and reader-printer positions will require 30 square feet each if machines are placed on tables. In 42-inch-wide carrells each microfiche reading station will take 35 square feet. A minimum of 250 square feet of staff space is also needed.

The most essential requirements for any microform area are environmental. The relative humidity should be maintained at from 40 to 50 percent and the temperature should be maintained near 70 degrees F. If microform gets too damp mold can form on it, causing damage to the photographic image over a long period of time. Dry film can become brittle and crack—although film stored in areas as low as 15 percent humidity can usually be successfully restored by an expert.

Most libraries are limited by the general air conditioning systems of their buildings. There are extreme conditions that warrant the addition of special equipment in the microform area. If the humidity is consistently low or high or is subject to rapid changes, a humidifier and/or dehumidifier should be installed. The dehumidifier is much more essential. Humidity over 60 percent for a sustained period of time is not at all uncommon in much of North America and definitely damaging.

Dehumidifiers using crystals of calcium chloride or other desiccants should not be used because they often give off fine dust particles that can abrade or bleach the microform. Low humidity is usually not permanently damaging unless it remains at below 15 percent for an extended period of time. Only libraries in arid regions need to concern themselves with that problem. Water trays and chemical solutions for increasing humidity should not be used because there is too little control over the amount of humidity produced. They can actually create excessively humid conditions inside a storage cabinet. A supplementary air conditioning unit should also be considered if the temperature rises over 80 degrees F regularly or if the temperature is subject to rapid changes.

Film can be as easily destroyed by water as books. Microform storage should, therefore, not be underneath water pipes or in an area that has fire sprinklers unless they are sheltered from the water. A reasonably dust-free environment is also important. Regular cleaning of the machines and periodic vacuuming of the storage equipment is necessary. If special air conditioning is installed, the incorporation of an electrostatic air filter to remove particulate matter from the air is a good idea.

Acoustic control is important because of machine noise and the movement of people in what will be a relatively densely populated area—the occupancy rate of microform areas tends to be much closer to capacity than regular reading areas. Not only should acoustic tile be used on the ceilings, but walls should be covered with a sound absorbant material. Wall carpeting is particularly effective and attractive. In addition to absorbing sound it helps reduce glare in a room, a major source of problems in a microform area. Floors should also be carpeted. If there is a local restriction of carpeting, the use of cork or another sound absorbing flooring material should be considered.

No special fire precautions are needed because virtually all commercially distributed film is slow burning. There should, nevertheless, be a no smoking rule and fire extinguishers should be on hand—the type which are recommended for electrical fires.

The author does not believe in dark microform reading rooms. That was necessary at one time when many front projection viewers with small wattage bulbs and without light hoods were in use. Today's equipment is designed to be used in modern offices and libraries with normal lighting. Glare is the problem today. It is encountered when machines are placed so that direct exterior light is reflected off the screens. It may also be a problem when light fixtures are reflected on the screens. The vertical screens of rear projection readers are particularly subject to external light and floor/table lamp reflections. The horizontal screens of front projection readers are most likely to reflect ceiling lights.

Drapes or blinds on the windows and proper placement of machines are usually all that is necessary to deal with glare problems.

Some patrons cannot be convinced that microform readers no longer require dark rooms. It is, therefore, a good idea when the library has a number of machines to place one or more of them in a very dimly lit area to be responsive to user opinion.

The layout of a microform area should be simple. It must be possible for a newcomer to understand the basic arrangement upon entering. The zones of activity which should be apparent are the reading area, reading machine area, service desk, duplicating area, and display area.

Reading Area

Regular library carrells with a surface of 2 by 3 feet (24 by 36 inches) are not adequate as bases for desktop microform readers. They just do not allow enough space to place books and other belongings and to take notes. If the machine is pushed to one side, usually to the left, left handed persons will be seriously inconvenienced. Many libraries feel their resources are too limited to purchase large carrells that measure 2 by 3.5 feet (24 by 42 inches). They want to use equipment which they already have. If that is the case, long tables of 6 to 8 feet in length are better than carrells. The machines should be placed on the tables in an alternating pattern so that the back of one machine fits between the backs of the two other machines on the other side of the table (fig. 4.1).

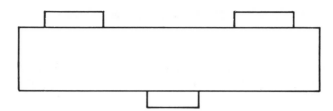

Fig. 4.1

In this way a machine can be placed each 3 to 4 feet (depending on whether it is a fiche or roll film machine) and still allow room on both sides for writing.

The major advantage of tables is that each machine can be allocated as much space as is needed. Some machines are only 15 inches wide while others are as much as 30 inches wide. Carrells are much less flexible in this regard. The major advatage of the carrells over the tables is that the former have full "returns" and provide the visual privacy which serious researchers like when they are working for several hours. Again, alternating the placement of machines on tables can provide some of this visual screening.

Carrells are usually arranged in rows, with all of them facing in the same direction. There is an alternative arrangement that provides greater visual privacy for readers. An alternating pattern has every other carrell facing in the opposite direction. Yet another pattern is a swastikalike four-carrell cluster.

Some institutions have spent a great deal of money to develop customized carrells that can be adjusted so that the reader can have the machine at the height and angle best for him or her. Interviews conducted with staff and patrons at one such library revealed that the adjustments are seldom made. A much less expensive solution is the use of secretarial chairs with posture adjustment for both height and angle. The author has also found that a small strip of wood can be inserted under the front or rear of a machine to change the angle just a few degrees for a patron who is uncomfortable.

Strips of plug-mold can be fastened to the underside of the carrells or tables to carry electrical power to the machines. The plug-mold can be fed from below the floor, from building columns, or from the ceiling above by suspending some attractive chrome tubes.

Printing Area

Regular reader-printers can be dispersed throughout the reading area or grouped together. If a machine is to be used solely for printing it should be placed near the service desk where the activity around the machine will be less distracting to patrons in the reading area. The print-only machines might well be coin-operated. A change machine might be provided in the very active microform area. The author has found it advisable to place print-only machines on standing height tables and provide no chairs. The space per machine should still be planned at 35 square feet, however, because there may be someone waiting in addition to the user of the machine. If the library is using regular reader-printers for printing only, they will be quite slow. Under those circumstances a tall stool should be available for the use of patrons with extensive copying. Ideally a production speed machine should be available because the only thing more frustrating than using a slow machine to make a large number of copies is waiting for someone who is making a large number of copies.

Storage Area

If the storage area is to be closed to the public it should be placed behind the service desk. It should be as square as possible to avoid staff having to travel the entire length of a rectangular space. It should be arranged so that the most frequently used materials are nearest the service area.

If the storage area is to be open to the public, it should be set up to allow movement from the reading area to the adjacent storage area without passing a large number of other reading positions. In other words, two parallel rectangular areas of reading and storage should be planned so that one need never pass through more than the width of the reading area.

The storage area should have a greater minimum floor loading than a conventional bookstack, 170 pounds per square foot, rather than 150 pounds per square foot. It should be planned for substantial expansion and with a view toward avoiding the future shifting of storage cabinets or stacks. A fully loaded floor 11-drawer storage cabinet with a companion unit on top of it weighs approximately 1,100 pounds. Emptying, shifting, and refilling cabinets is costly and time consuming. If a closed area is definitely to remain closed somewhat narrower aisles can be used than in an open access collection, but if there is any chance that the storage area will be opened to the patrons—and the trend is definitely in that direction—it is wise to plan the wider public aisles.

Microform storage areas lend themselves to the use of electromechanical compact storage even if direct patron access is provided.

In some libraries the microform master copies are also shelved in the microform area. These are the originals from which the service or reference copies have been made. In most libraries the masters would be of local newspapers or archival materials. The author recommends against storing these in the same location as the service copies because everything could be destroyed in a fire or flood. It may also result in staff using a master copy periodically when the service copy is not available.

Staff Area

The staff must be accommodated near the entrance to the area. It should be highly visible to persons walking into the area. The service desk should control the storage area in a closed stacks collection and yet it should have good visual control of the reading area, not just to protect materials and machines, but also to identify patrons who may need assistance. The catalog of the collection should also be placed near the entry for the public and for easy access by the staff.

If there is a desk rather than a counter, additional storage should be provided for portable microform readers, paper for the reader-printers, and other supplies which will be needed in the reading area. A work room is absolutely essential. There must be a place for inspecting, cleaning, and repairing microform. Repair of microform is not a simple operation. It requires special equipment, materials, and skills. It cannot be properly done by an attendant sitting at a public service desk.

Equipment in the work room should include a film inspection and splicing desk with a light box for examining microform, a rewinder for roll film, and a splicing machine. Some storage space for microform being handled should be provided. There should also be storage space for microform supplies, including basic spare parts for the machines. If a film cleaner is owned, it might be housed here.

Notes

1. Holmes, Donald C. "Determination of User Needs and Future Requirements for a Systems Approach to Microform Technology." Washington, D.C.: Association of Research Libraries, 1969 (ERIC Document ED 029 168).

2. Spreitzer, Francis F. "Report to the Council on Library Resources," 1975 (unpublished).

5
OPTICAL MEDIA

There are a number of emerging technologies that may be suitable for library and information center applications. All of them claim greater storage capacity, faster information retrieval, support of multiple concurrent users, and lower costs than existing media such as magnetic storage and microform. The most publicized of the new technologies are the optical media: videodisc, compact disc, CD-ROM, and optical digital storage (on disk, tape, and cards). These technologies share "optical" characteristics in that the encoding of information on each medium relies on the use of optically sensitive materials; most also use light—generally in the form of lasers—for both recording and reading.

The materials and processes underlying each medium are remarkably similar; the differences arise from the ways in which the media are being developed and marketed for commercial applications. These applications are undergoing continued change as companies that have expended billions of dollars in developing the technology continue to reshape their product lines in search of what is proving to be an elusive market.

In 1986, four types of optical media were being promoted in North America: videodisc, compact audio disc, CD-ROM, and optical disks. Each of these will be discussed in turn.

Videodisc

The videodisc is a circular plastic platter, generally twelve inches in diameter, with a central spindle hole and an exposed shiny, rainbow-hued, mirrorlike surface. Information is recorded as pits or bubbles on an optically sensitive surface protected by a plastic overlay. Each pit or bubble is about 1/50th of the width of a human hair, allowing information to be recorded in very high densities.

The term "videodisc" is misleading insofar as it suggests that the disc is strictly a video medium, a technology displayed through a television receiver for entertainment or instructional purposes. The terminology is appropriate in that the distinguishing characteristic of the videodisc is that all information is recorded within the audio and video format of a standard television signal. The medium is not limited, however, to the reproduction of moving images and sound; it will accommodate still images and digital data.

Motion and still video, audio, and digital data may be mixed on a single disc, or a disc may be devoted to only one type of data. Applications that combine audio and video programming are the most firmly established; but programming that mixes audio, video, and digital data on a single disc is becoming commonplace. As of mid-1986 it was still uncommon for a videodisc to be devoted entirely to digital data. The best known product in this format was LSSI's MiniMARC, a standalone cataloging support system.

When used only for video storage, a single videodisc can accommodate 54,000 frames per side.

Of several competing types of videodisc, the reflective optical videodisc is dominant, and commercial support for other videodisc technologies had virtually disappeared. Although some services support the production of single or limited quantity discs, the dominant use of the videodisc technology is in applications which require the mass replication of many copies of a disc.

In addition to offering linear, sequential playback of video and audio programming, videodisc systems offer a variety of other capabilities, including:

- slow motion
- fast motion, in forward or reverse
- freeze frame, when the action is stopped at one among many frames of a motion sequence
- still frame, achieved through display of a single frame of text, art, or photograph, designed specifically for use

in the still frame mode of play, or by displaying a series of identical frames of a single nonaction image. The technical requirements for each type of still frame display differ with the formatting of true still frame material requiring special care in preparation of the program material.

- scan, in forward or reverse. In scan mode, a player skips over several tracks at a time, displaying only a fraction of the frames it passes. This mode is analogous to skimming through the pages of a book.

Besides normal play and scanning, many videodisc systems offer a third method of access: a search or random access function. Players that support this feature have input keys on the machine itself or on a remote control keypad. By entering the number of the required frame the user can retrieve it with accuracy in seconds.

The most successful application of the videodisc has been as a publishing and distribution medium for general purpose "entertainment" programs such as motion pictures, and as the vehicle for interactive programs for training, education, arcade games, public information, and marketing.

A number of institutions with large pictorial archives, including the Library of Congress and the Smithsonian's National Air and Space Museum, are storing still and motion images on videodisc. The technology, however, has not yet proved adaptable for the routine recording and displaying of frames of still text such as pages of books and journal articles. The standard television equipment used for videodisc systems is poorly suited to the display of text. A regular television screen has 250,000 pixels or dots of resolution. To be legible, the image of a printed page needs to be displayed on a screen with between 500,000 and 1 million pixels. High resolution television receivers that meet this requirement are available, but they are expensive.

The standard videodisc format is designed to handle video images at resolution akin to those supported by regular receiver technology. Within these limits a standard television screen can legibly display only 1,200 or so characters—20 lines of approximately 60 characters per line. Thus, in most circumstances, the simple capture and storage of page images on videodisc formatted in accordance with North American television standards will not produce an acceptable display.

A number of companies have developed techniques for capturing and replicating machine-readable data on videodisc. Products aimed at the library market are at the vanguard of this application. Library Systems & Services Inc. had replicated the entire LC MARC data base on two videodiscs to support the MiniMARC cataloging support system.

While most of the applications that use videodisc for the storage of text utilize a direct video approach, the IIT Research Institute (IITRI) of Chicago is pursuing a variant procedure in which page images are reformatted and displayed on standard television monitors/receivers. In the IITRI Videodisc Production System (IVPS) a high-resolution television camera is used to digitize a page image at a resolution of 4 million pixels per page. The scanned image is examined by a computer and "decomposed" into a layout suited for display on a television screen. The software locates columns, breaks between words, spaces between lines, etc., and determines the pieces or screens into which the page is to be decomposed. The text is rearranged so as to provide a series of screens of intelligible, readable, sequential text. Each such screen is recorded as a standard television signal which is captured for mastering on videodisc.

The decomposed image is a facsimile of the original page in terms of type font and print style. It varies from the original only with regard to layout and spacing. IVPS is used to produce black and white images. Early research suggested that a standard 8-1/2 × 11-inch page could be satisfactorily decomposed into an average of 5.3 frames per page, more recent work indicates that an average of 12 frames per page is required. At 12 frames per page, one side of a videodisc with a capacity of 54,000 frames can accommodate only 4,500 print pages. The IVPS system had been used successfully to process certain types of tables and schematics as well as regular text.

There is also considerable research in recording digital data on videodisc. Two methods are being pursued: in both, the digital data is mastered and replicated in quantity runs using commercial videodisc production facilities and procedures.

The first approach—digital dumps—accommodates only limited amounts of data and is generally used to record player control instructions on interactive videodiscs designed for use with programmable videodisc players. A more recent development—the premastering of digital data on videotape—allows vast quantities of digital data to be recorded, and replicated, on videodisc. Any type of digital data may be "published" in this way, including machine-searchable ASCII coded alpha-numerics, bit-mapped image data, and digitized audio data.

The Lister Hill National Center for Biomedical Communications of the National Library of Medicine was a pioneer in developing techniques for the recording of large quantities of digital information on a videodisc and its playback on a regular industrial videodisc player. This work was eclipsed when a Massachusetts-based company, LaserData, developed a proprietary method of converting digital data into the analog codes used on videodisc. The LaserData technique is based on research undertaken by MIT.

Using this technique, a videodisc with a capacity of 54,000 frames per side can accommodate up to 1.2 billion characters, or 1.2 GB, of digital data. The actual amount of usable storage depends upon the error detection and correction techniques applied. Different techniques are promoted by the various companies now active in this field—LaserData, Reference Technology Inc. (RTI), TMS Inc., etc. Although the procedures for publishing digital data in this format have been available for some time, applications are only now being brought to the market. The reports from MiniMARC users have been encouraging.

Some problems are expected. Paramount among these is the identification and correction of errors. Mastering and replication procedures for videodisc production do not allow dynamic error identification and correction. There are many sources of errors in the production process, including errors in mastering and replication, and errors due to flaws in the materials used in disc production. Errors occur in the production of videodiscs for entertainment purposes. These errors, while often visible, are seldom obtrusive to the eye or ear. The sensitivity of machine-readable information to errors is much greater, since the loss or change of a single bit could cause a computer program to malfunction, or an index to return wrong information.

The future of the videodisc for text applications was uncertain as of mid-1986 and there was little prospect that libraries and information centers will within the next few years be able to scan books, journals, photographs, and other materials with the intent of preserving the information on videodisc. The use of the videodisc for the storage of digital data appeared more firmly established, but likely to be challenged by CD-ROM applications.

Compact Disc

The compact disc being promoted by the music industry share many aspects of the technology used in videodiscs. The compact disc technology promoted by Philips and Sony uses optical laser recording techniques and optical playback systems similar to those developed for reflective optical videodiscs. The compact disc is replicated using similar mastering and stamping techniques. A 4-3/4 inch one-sided compact audio disc provides one hour of high quality stereo playback.

While conceptually similar, there is one major difference between a compact disc and a video disc: the nature of the signal which is recorded. A video disc stores information in an analog television format. All data—image, audio, or digital—has to be converted to this format during the remastering process. By contrast, a compact audio disc is geared to the encoding of audio data directly in digital form.

Like the videodisc technology, the compact disc is being promoted primarily—in fact, as of mid-1986, solely—as a mass replication technology. A master is produced and copies are stamped out on high speed equipment. As of mid-1986 compact disc production facilities were available only in Germany and Japan. The first U.S. facility was scheduled to become operational in late 1986.

The only application of the compact disc is high quality audio reproduction. More than 50 percent of all classical music sales is now in the format. The technology is expected to displace phonodisc and cassette tape in another decade.

While any type of digital data may be mastered and replicated on a compact disc, including video and ASCII characters, the terms "compact disc" is almost exclusively used to refer to discs that carry digitized audio data. Almost all of the research into the technology involves consumer audio applications. As of mid-1986 there appeared little prospect that the technology would be adapted to video or image storage.

CD-ROM

A separate technology—also using a small reflective optical disc—was emerging in 1986: CD-ROM (compact disc read-only memory). While it uses the same medium as compact disc technology, the initiative has come from the computer industry rather than from the recording industry. Development priorities and marketing approaches are, therefore, quite different. Although CD-ROM drives—the equivalent of the audio players— were not available in commercial quantities at the beginning of 1986, there was considerable interest in this use of the medium, and by the end of the year it appeared that ample supplies would be available.

CD-ROM is replicated from a master disk using techniques comparable to those used in producing videodiscs and compact audio discs. The capacity of a single CD-ROM is approximately 550 million characters (550 MB).

The major application of CD-ROM technology is as a read-only publishing format for machine-readable data. The small size of the medium and the disk player makes it particularly well suited to personal and desk top computers. A CD-ROM drive will actually fit into the same space as a floppy disk drive. The relatively slow retrieval speed—one second or more— also makes it desirable to use the CD-ROM only on single user systems.

For electronic publishing applications, text can be recorded in digital form in two ways: (1) the image of a printed page can be digitized as a pattern of light and dark marks, or (2) the text can be encoded character-by-character in the standard digital representation of each alphabetic or numeric character. Applied to a standard typed page, the image scanning method results in the generation of some 32 KB of data. (Scanning of more densely packed printed pages requires high resolutions and consequently greater data loads.) Recording the contents of the typed page by coding the individual characters in digital code would generate only four KB of information. A byte takes the same amount of storage regardless of the method by which it was generated.

In addition to being more compact, data input in coded form, one character at a time, can also be searched that way. So a page of *Business Week* input as coded characters can be accessed by a keyword search. For example, a search could be conducted for the words "optical" and "disk" when they occur in proximity to one another anywhere on a page. The search would retrieve that part of the text that contains these key words. Digitized page images cannot be searched in this way. However, there are applications in which a producer might choose to store data as page images rather than in character encoded form. Image scanning can be faster and less expensive than machine coding; pictorial and other graphic information can be retained in image scanning; and, if undertaken at a sufficiently high resolution, the digitally scanned page can be reproduced as an exact facsimile of the original document on a printer or a high-resolution screen.

A number of electronic publishing projects were emerging in 1986, but the only one was sufficiently established for evaluation—Bibliofile, The Library Corporation's cataloging support system. Bibliofile offers the LC MARC data base encoded on three CD-ROM. A library or information center provides the personal computer and purchases the CD-ROM drive, the personal computer interface, cabling, and applications software for $2,390. An annual subscription to quarterly deliveries of the cumulative data base was less than $1,500. Some 100 systems had been installed and appeared to be working satisfactorily.

As of mid-1986 developments in the use of CD-ROM appeared to be progressing far more rapidly than efforts to record digital information on videodisc. One reason is that two of the companies that developed the technology—N. V. Philips and Sony—reached early agreement on formatting standards and have influenced the entire industry. A one-sided CD-ROM disk, which adheres to these standards has a storage capacity of 550 MB and can be played on any player from any manufacturer. In contrast, five incompatible videodisc technologies have been developed. The emphasis in CD-ROM research appeared to be on the publishing of machine-readable data bases.

At present North American applications are being inhibited by the absence of production facilities on the continent.

Optical Digital Storage

The fourth group of optical devices are generally known as optical digital data storage media. While most commonly utilizing a disk format, there are also tape and card formats. The media share common technological foundations with videodisc, compact disc, and CD-ROM. The essential difference is again one of the targeted application and the consequent direction of commercial development.

Most work on the optical digital disk, the most popular format, has been directed toward the computer mass storage market. The intent is to develop a computer storage peripheral capable of augmenting traditional magnetic disks and, possibly, replacing magnetic tape media. Success in this market is dependent upon the storage medium being able to record data at the user site and being as easily written as read. This is in marked contrast to the direction of product developments for the videodisc, compact disc, and CD-ROM—all of which emphasize mass replication and read-only applications. The optical digital media stress write-once-and-read capabilities—also called DRAW (direct-read-after-write).

Write-once and multiple-read characteristics make the optical digital media quite different from magnetic disk and tape. The magnetic media are erasable and thus provide both multiple-write and multiple-read capabilities. While many companies are attempting to engineer erasability into optical digital media, as of mid-1986 these attempts had not resulted in anything more tangible than prototype systems and tentative product announcements.

The greatest advantage of the optical digital technologies is storage capacity. Devices capable of storing 4 GB of data on one side of a 14-inch optical digital disk are now available. The actual capacity of the disk is greater, but between 20 and 50 percent of storage is typically devoted to data formatting and error detection and correction requirements.

Among the attractions of the media for computer mass

storage applications are environmental considerations such as the relatively compact size of an optical storage system, the tolerant temperature and humidity requirements, and the lack of susceptibility of the medium to magnetic, electrical, and other types of interference. As is the case in relation to the predominantly read-only optical media of videodisc and compact disc, discussion of the comparative advantages of optical digital media is clouded by the variety of different systems being developed. This is exacerbated by differences in the performance characteristics of laboratory and custom developed systems and those relatively few products which are currently available in the commercial market.

Market penetration of the optical digital media has been disappointing. In North America, the media were slow to get established. It was only in the second half of 1984 that deliverable systems became a reality and in mid-1986 most of the usage still appeared to be experimental, and such usage as there was, was far below the levels projected by most industry analysts.

At least one library application appeared imminent in 1986. CLSI, the vendor of automated local library systems planned to make its CL-Medline available on optical digital discs attached to a microVAX computer. The data base would be transferred from magnetic tape to optical discs using equipment at the company's home office. The libraries with CL-Medline systems would receive periodic disc shipments for mounting on their optical digital disc drives. At least two installations were scheduled for late 1986.

Optical digital storage research in Europe appeared as of late 1986 to be focused on the development of large storage systems. In Japan the focus was on very small systems suitable for attachment to word processing equipment. There was not yet a basis for determining whether libraries and information centers would be able to make effective use of the media. Nevertheless, the large capacity of the media and the DRAW capability held out promise that this approach might be adaptable to in-house scanning and recording of printed text and graphics.

It is as yet too soon to be able to predict the economics and other practicalities of such usage of optical digital storage. In 1986 the Library of Congress was performing a detailed investigation of the scanning, storage, and retrieval of digitized images of journal articles on optical digital disk. No formal evaluation report has yet been issued but certain aspects of the project were said to be problematic. These included nontechnology-related factors such as document preparation, retrieval indexing, and copyright. It is believed that some problems were also being encountered with the technology.

Future Prospects

A number of the optical technologies may have a future in libraries and information centers. In fact, some are already being used. Many public libraries have expanded their collections to encompass motion picture programming on videodisc and sound recordings on compact audio disc; and academic and special libraries are also being called upon to provide access to interactive videodisc programs for education and training.

At the next level of sophistication, the preservation and access opportunities that videodisc and compact disc offer for video and audio materials currently published in other formats were being explored in 1986. Examples of such usage of the technologies are relatively few: the National Air and Space Museum's videodisc collection of photographs of the history of aviation; the Library of Congress's compact disc of music performances from its collection; and the Library of Congress's videodisc transfer of motion picture footage previously available only as paper prints.

Several organizations were beginning to market machine-readable data bases published on videodisc or CD-ROM to libraries and information centers in 1986. Most of these data bases had previously been available only through large online computer systems—in-house systems or remote systems accessed through increasingly expensive telecommunications channels. The economics of the optical media, and their ability to give data base producers direct access to users without the mediation of a data base service, has provided even small data base producers with a unique marketing opportunity. For example, The Library Corporation, a company with sales of only a few hundred thousand dollars a year, is marketing Bibliofile, a cataloging support system utilizing the complete Library of Congress MARC file on CD-ROM. At least a dozen other data base producers are actively pursuing the direct delivery of their data bases to end users on digitally encoded videodisc or CD-ROM.

Videodisc will probably remain the most desirable medium for still and motion video through the eighties. Compact disc will probably dominate the audio market by the end of the decade. As yet, it is not clear whether any one of the optical media offer significant advantages over the others in mass replication applications for digital data such as the distribution of software, bibliographic data, and digitized full-text data bases. Videodisc has an advantage when an application includes a mix of digital data and analog video or image data, and it currently offers a greater storage capacity than CD-ROM. CD-ROM offers simpler production techniques, and the promise of more widely available and less expensive retrieval equipment.

Although production costs are falling, it is not yet clear whether the relatively high initial mastering cost of the videodisc and CD-ROM will make it possible to use the technologies for applications in which only a few copies are required. The DRAW disk, which was beginning to become generally available in North America in 1986, may be the more suitable technology when a single copy or a limited number of copies are required. Using the DRAW process, only one disk is made at a time, unless several recording units are placed side by side and used simultaneously. Conceptually, there is no reason why DRAW disks cannot be replicated in quantity. Indeed, at least one manufacturer of write-once systems mentions this possibility in its product literature. In 1986, however, this capability was not being pursued by the industry.

Libraries and information centers are not likely to have a major impact on product development. The driving applications in which the disk is used as the storage medium—especially for digitized images—are likely to be in commercial organizations which have access as their primary motivation. The technology's ability to reduce large paper and microfiche files to a single compact form, readily and rapidly accessible from multiple local or remote workstations, is attractive to enterprises such as banks and insurance companies. Banks and insurance companies usually require hundreds of copies of each file as contrasted with the libraries and information centers which usually require only one. All organizations can appreciate the fact that systems based on the optical technologies entail no manual refiling and do not involve one-at-a-time limitations on use.

A major factor in the suitability of the optical technologies is the relatively high up-front cost for producing a master before service copies are replicated. To the extent that preservation involves the production of one or a limited number of copies, the unit costs may be high; to the extent that an emphasis on access may involve the production of many copies, the unit costs may be low. A republisher is, therefore, likely to choose those titles that are likely to sell hundreds or thousands of copies, rather than those that will sell 100 or fewer copies.

The publishing industry will probably adopt videodisc and CD-ROM for two kinds of publishing ventures: data base publishing and republishing. Since both technologies require the creation of a master and replication by one of a handful of service bureaus, it is expected that the optimim quantities will be 1,000 to 5,000 copies. As of mid-1986 the more than 50 announced products were almost all reference publications expected to get heavy use, but at least one republisher was working on a journal republication program. The focus was on recent titles in business and technology—those which special libraries now purchase on microform in lieu of binding, but which they don't retain for more than five years or so. No publisher or republisher appeared to be pursuing the preservation market.

All of the optical media offer potential for libraries and information centers, but when compared with the alternatives of microform and paper, the present limited archival life—10 years guaranteed, although 30 can reasonably be expected—of the media will retard their adoption. It will be necessary either to increase life expectancy will beyond the present ten year estimates or to set up master files on more stable or readily monitored media from which new copies can be generated as required. The industry will have to decide that archivability is a high priority for the former to come about. The latter will depend on well established republishers and library and information center consortia with the resources and stability to make long-term commitments.

As of 1986 it did not appear that libraries and information centers would be able to shift their focus from microform for at least the next few years, It would appear to be desirable, however, to limit the investment in micrographics and to anticipate the future installation of retrieval devices of optically stored data.

The use of DRAW technology as an alternative to CAR appears attractive, but the only available systems are prototypes. As of 1986 it would cost $115,000 to equal the capacity of a $75,000 CAR system. Lower priced production models are expected within two years.

Space Requirements

The technologies are still quite new, but it is now possible to spell out general requirements for the optical media.

Analog videodiscs are likely to be mounted on table model disc players that can be installed in any carrell or other study station which is wide enough to accommodate the equipment without displacing writing space. The traditional width of 3 feet should be increased to 4 feet. Electrical power should also be provided. The typical unit draws no more than 2 AMPS and can share a circuit with other equipment, provided that there are no large motors on the circuit.

Digitally encoded videodiscs may be used as either a peripheral to a personal micro or a multiuser system. In the former case, a working surface of at least 30 by 72 inches should be planned. As a peripheral to an integrated library system, a drive will require less space than the magnetic drives now in common use. They are less likely to displace them, however, than to augment them. The faster magnetic drives will probably continue to support local bibliographic files and the larger, slower optical media such as digital videodisc and optical digital disk will probably contain resource data bases, full-text files, etc. The computer room should, therefore, be planned with additonal space for one or more digital videodisc drives. See Chapter 3 for details.

It appears likely that CD-ROM devices will be attached to personal computers, rather than to the larger computer at a library's central site. The planning requirements for micro-based workstations would, therefore, be suitable for the medium.

Each carrell or desk should, therefore, be a foot wider than the traditional width to accommodate the equipment. There should also be provision for bringing power to the CD-ROM drive. See Chapter 3 for details.

The optical digital disk is most likely to be used as a peripheral device on a multi-user system, either the same computer as the library uses in its integrated library system or a separate one interconnected with it. The site preparation requirements for a central computer room set forth in Chapter 3 would, therefore, apply.

6

TELEFACSIMILE

Paperless society forecasts are common, but they overlook the fact that the bulk of any library or information center's resources will continue to be in printed form for decades to come. The existing holdings of a library or information center represent a tremendous investment. An organization is rarely in a position to spend millions of dollars to reformat these resources from print to machine-readable form. In addition, the copyright holders of published materials may resist such reformatting. The publishing community is generally conservative with regard to technology. University Microfilms International (UMI), a major microform republisher, is experiencing considerable difficulty obtaining permission to reformat materials to electronic formats from the 8,000 journal publishers with whom it has sought to negotiate. Since UMI is proposing to deal with the problems of the technology and the economics, UMI's conclusion that the traditional publisher is still very much concerned about losing control of copyrighted material when it is in electronic form appears sound.

As suggested in Chapter 2, it may take several more years before a substantial percentage of the information libraries and information centers seek to collect is in machine-readable form. In a major unpublished study of the impact of 14 technologies on academic library space planning funded by the State University System of Florida, the author concluded that new technology would augment rather than displace printed materials through the 1990s. At least for the next 20 years libraries will have to be designed with room for books, journals, and readers at tables. But there will also have to be room for electronic devices.

As libraries increase their reliance on electronic transmission of bibliographic and full-text information, there is likely to be a growing demand for printed materials to be moved among libraries more rapidly than now. While libraries and information centers have substantially mastered the complexity of verifying citations, accessing files of millions of records to identify holding locations and rapidly transmitting loan requests; the actual movement of the information has not been improved. In fact, the actual movement of materials may be slower than before the adoption of electronic technology to facilitate the location and requesting process.

The document delivery problem appears to affect all interlibrary loan activities irrespective of the location, distance, or type of material involved. Despite an expectation that distance is a significant factor in delivery costs and thus a prime contributor to the document delivery deadlock, the dilemma is as pressing for libraries in the Greater New York area wishing to share their resources as for those in the Far West involved in loans with the Eastern Seaboard. While there is some evidence to suggest that the movement of an average 10-page journal article is slightly faster than that of a much bulkier monograph, current interlibrary lending practices do not appear to achieve significantly better delivery times for photocopies.

The problem is clear: how to achieve the efficient delivery of interlibrary loan materials within the dual but opposing constraints of economy and speed?

While the use of Library Rate postage is economically attractive—$.54 for the first pound and $.19 for each additional pound up to seven pounds—it is a disaster timewise, with postal officials quoting 10 to 12 days for a distance of 1,000 miles. A photocopy of an average 10-page journal article (2 ounces) may be sent by First Class Mail for a cost of $.39 with an expected delivery time of three days over a distance greater than 1,000 miles when other than major cities are involved. A two-pound Priority Mail package—the fastest regular service for packages over 16 ounces—would cost $2.40 over the same distance, but it would be four or five days before delivery.

Where the volume of materials movement warrants it, the establishment of a courier services dedicated to the movement of library and information center materials is an attractive option. The cost calculation for such an arrangement should include not only the commonly considered costs of salaries and fuel, but also overhead such as driver benefits and backup, vehicle depreciation, and insurance. The experience varies widely, but few organizations claim to deliver for less than $2.50 per item.

Given the current state of information technology, three alternatives to regular mail service and local library courier systems have been tried: U.S. Postal Service Express Mail, commercial courier services, and telefacsimile.

Of the various "overnight" delivery services, the Express Mail system operated by the U.S. Postal Service is the least expensive, offering "next day" delivery at $10.75 for a package up to two pounds—the same price for a brief article or a typical monograph. The price is independent of distance. Even if cost were no object, Express Mail would not offer a total solution to the document delivery problem as items have to be presented at designated Express Mail dispatch points and the service does not apply to many destinations.

The commercial courier services that offer overnight delivery are normally quite expensive for books, with rates averaging more than double those of Express Mail. For organizations that send more than two overnight envelopes a day, the rate for sending a journal article is $9.00 or less. United Parcel Service, a surface carrier with varying rates depending on distance, charges $1.25 to $2.50 for a journal article or monograph delivered within 400 miles. Most deliveries within such distances are completed the next day. United Parcel Service would, therefore, be the lowest cost service offering rapid delivery within a distance of 400 miles. For greater distances the cost remains low, but delivery times stretch to three to five days.

All of these options cost almost the same for a few pages or an entire monograph. What is needed is a rapid, cost effective alternative for the delivery of photocopies of journal articles and excerpts from monographs. For this application high speed telefacsimile equipment is becoming increasingly popular. It bypasses both the delays of regular mail and the costs of Express Mail and courier services for interlibrary loans that involve 20 pages or fewer.

Telefacsimile Defined

Telefacsimile is an image oriented electronic technology that is used to transmit and reconstitute full pages of text—in roman or nonroman alphabets—drawings, or illustrations over a tele-communications medium. The terms "telefacsimile," "facsimile," and "fax" are interchangeable. Telefacsimile has had a relatively poor reputation in the library and business communities because most of the organizations' experiences have been with the older analog machines that transmit slowly—between two and six minutes for a single typewritten page—and with relatively poor image resolution. New, fast, high-resolution digital telefacsimile equipment capable of transmitting a regular typed page in 15–60 seconds reduces the telecommunications costs of the medium while offering better quality output. The actual transmission time of a typeset page will vary from 50 seconds to two minutes depending on the nature of the text and the graphic material, and the resolution at which the transmission is made.

Using digital equipment with a speed of 30 seconds per page, a 20-page transcontinental transmission could be completed for a cost of less than $8.00, compared with a charge of $90.40 if using a six-minute-per-page analog machine. The resolution achieved with digital fax is nearly as good as that of a photocopy, depending on the nature of the text and the graphic material, and the resolution at which the transmission is made. The quality of an analog transmission is poor, similar to that of a television image.

Digital telefacsimile machines usually cost from $2,000 to $12,000 each (rental $120 to $600 per month) as compared with analog machines at $1,700 each (rental approximately $80 per month). Higher equipment cost can be offset, however, by reduced operator involvement and the lower telecommunications costs realized by using the higher speed digital devices.

Volume of Activity

The volume of activity is a critical factor in the decision to use digital telefacsimile for document delivery and in the choice of equipment. A low-volume machine is one that is expected to be used to transmit fewer than 500 pages per month; a medium-range machine would be for 500 to 1,000 pages per month; and a high-volume machine for more than 1,000 pages per month. Assuming that a high-volume digital machine can be rented for $400 per month, that supplies cost under $.04 per page, and that the daytime line cost for a 2,500 mile transmission is $.54 for the first minute and $.38 for each additional minute, the transmission of 100 pages each month using a digital machine would cost $454 for the month ($4.54 per page). The picture changes dramatically if 1000 pages are transmitted. The cost of the transmission becomes $940 for the month ($.94 per page). By using a discounted long-distance service and calling during off-peak periods this cost can be reduced to as little as $.60 per page. Within a local calling area in which message units are charged the cost per page—if a volume of 1,000 pages a month is assumed—would be approximately $.55 per page.

Resolution

Copy resolution is determined by the number of lines per inch (1pi) measured vertically. Typed documents are legible at 64 lpi. Most analog machines offer this degree of resolution. Digital machines usually offer resolutions of 67, 100, and 200 lpi; often described as high-speed, standard, and detail modes respectively. The detail mode offers slightly less resolution than the typical office photocopier. Nippon Electric Company (NEC) offers a machine (the first of the so-called Group IV machines) with a superfine resolution option (400 lpi) that can also be used as a regular office copier—at somewhat higher per copy cost than most office copiers. In a recent test of high speed facsimile approximately 90 percent of the materials transmitted by one major academic library over a period of two months were sent at standard resolution; only 10 percent required the use of the detail mode—primarily scientific articles with detailed formulas and graphics.

Transmission Speed

The transmission speed of computer terminals is usually expressed in "baud"—one baud being one signal element per second. With voice-grade telephone lines and regular modems the practical upper limit is 1,800 baud. Most libraries use 300 or 1,200 baud terminals with local library systems and for remote data base searching. Higher speed modems are normally incorporated into telefacsimile equipment. They achieve faster data transmission by encoding more data bits in a baud—a modem operating at 1,200 baud, but encoding two bits in a baud effectively transmits data at 2,400 bits per second (bps). Some modems will transmit data over voice-grade lines at 4,800 and 9,600 bps. Many digital machines transmit information at a speed of 9,600 bps. A penalty is paid for the very high speed in increased error rates. Because of that, it is common to limit transmission speeds over voice lines to 4,800 bits per second. Automatic stepdown or modem shiftdown, available on some digital fax units, allows the rate of transmission to be set at 9,600 and automatically reduced to 7,200 to 4,800 to 2,400 bps to improve copy quality as needed to compensate for transmission line problems and to adjust to other equipment which operates at lower transmission speeds.

Document Feeding

All telefacsimile machines accept only single sheet feed—typed, printed, or photocopied pages. In interlibrary loan applications the requested material has to be photocopied before being transmitted. This is already the case, however, in most journal article loans irrespective of the delivery method. Instead of sending the original photocopy to the requesting institution, it can be filed or discarded. Libraries that have had experience in faxing photocopies from bound journals have discovered that it is important to avoid wide black boundaries around the image because the fax machine will scan and transmit the dark area. In one institution the unwanted black area is trimmed off to reduce average transmission time to less than one minute per page.

Many fax machines have automatic feeding devices that will accept up to 40 or 50 sheets for dispatch. Machines so equipped need not be attended while transmitting to a single location although an operator has to be on hand to make the initial line connection. Automatic dialers remove the need for manual dialing and make it possible to schedule transmissions for periods of lowest telecommunication rates or for times when staff are not available to start the process. The higher price machines also offer delivery verification features so that the transmitting unit senses that the receiving unit has actually printed the copy.

Paper

Most telefacsimile machines use 300 paper roll in the receiving unit. It is usually 8.5 to 11 inches in width, but the maximum length of a single page can vary significantly from machine to machine. Two types of printers are used: thermal and electrostatic. The former requires special treated paper and the latter uses plain paper of the type now used in most medium to high-volume office copying machines. The feel of the treated paper varies a great deal. Some librarians have found that treated papers that do not look and feel like regular copy paper are unpopular with users even when the image is perfectly clear.

Transmission Media

Virtually all telefacsimile machines can transmit via voice grade unconditioned telephone lines—dial up or leased. Libraries are using WATS lines, MCI, and a variety of other long-distance services to reduce telecommunications costs. Experienced users of equipment without auto-dialers have added this feature to facilitate the dialing of the 22-digit numbers the use of the special services may require. The digital machines can also transmit via digital telephone lines or broadband media such as microwave, satellite, coaxial cable, or fiber optic cable.

Machine Compatibility

Compatibility among digital machines of different manufacturers can normally be achieved by stipulating that all equipment conform to the international standard of the Consultative Committee on International Telephone and Telegraph (CCITT) for Group 3 digital equipment; most analog machines conform to Group 1 or 2 standards. If the digital machines are required to be compatible with older analog equipment, downward compatibility to Group 1 and/or 2 equipment must be specified. When digital and analog machines are interfaced, the transmission is conducted at analog speeds and capacities. It is desirable to batch transmission to a particular machine because the first 10 to 15 seconds of each transmission is required for the equipment to establish the electronic "handshake" with the receiving unit.

There are at least 11 suppliers of high speed telefacsimile equipment in the United States, but only two offer at least six different pieces of equipment: Rapicom and 3M. Only NEC offers the new Group 4 equipment that includes 400 lpm resolution, very rapid transmission, and the ability to function as a universal printing device. The availability of an extensive and compatible equipment line from a single vendor provides the opportunity to assemble a network of machines with different characteristics to meet the requirements of various participants in a fax network from a single supplier. By buying from a single source quantity discounts and special service agreements may be negotiated and compatibility problems can be minimized. Most organizations, however, will not have the choice of specifying all of the equipment with which their machine(s) will communicate. They should not only specify compatibility with specific CCITT Groups, but should also confirm compatibility with machines already installed in organizations with which they intend to communicate regularly.

Space Requirements

A digital telefacsimile machine can be installed almost anywhere. At least 40 square feet should be provided. What is
required for optimum operations is a table surface of at least 2
by 4 feet (24 by 48 inches), a 15 AMP dedicated circuit, a telephone line, and a nearby photocopier for copying from bound
materials. In areas with erratic electrical power a power conditioner (surge protector) should be installed at the electrical
outlet. It is also a good idea to put an antistatic mat on the floor
in front of the machine. No special acoustical or humidity control requirements exist. The most common location is in the
interlibrary loan department. Other locations that are popular
are reference and circulation departments.

7
COMPACT STORAGE

While microform and optical mass storage technologies have—
and will continue to have—a significant impact on space planning for libraries and information centers, the continuing need
to maximize the storage capacity for materials in hardcopy must
not be overlooked. The technology known as "compact storage" serves that need. The technology consists of "compact
shelving," or movable ranges of shelving mounted on tracks
fastened to the floor and "compact filing," or storage bins hung
in a vertical carousel cabinet. The former is the more common
in libraries, the latter in offices.

Compact shelving saves space by eliminating unneces-
sary aisles. Instead of an aisle between each range, one aisle
serves a whole shelving module. By moving the ranges an aisle
is created wherever the needed material is located. While conventional shelving systems use one-third of the allotted floor
space for housing materials and two-thirds for access and aisle
space. Compact shelving, on the other hand, uses 80 percent
of the allotted floor space for housing materials and 20 percent
for access and aisle space. A typical large configuration is shown
in figure 7.1

In addition to gaining space, mobile shelving and filing
also increase security, since all units can be rolled together and
locked. Materials stored are also less subject to deterioration
because of light, dirt, and moisture. Mobile filing systems are
also popular because they eliminate much of the walking by
staff to retrieve information.

Most compact shelving installations are not large, but
consist of only a few ranges of shelving housing up to 10,000
less frequently used volumes. Initially the installations were
primarily in special libraries that occupied expensive space in

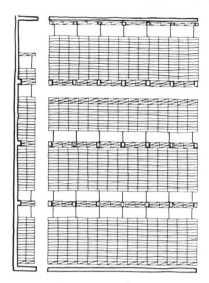

Fig. 7.1

office buildings. It has only been in the past few years that large academic and public libraries have begun to install systems that can accommodate hundreds of thousands of volumes.

Despite the dramatic increase in the use of compact shelving in the past few years, there is only a limited amount of information in the literature. This chapter, therefore, describes the compact shelving and filing technologies in detail as well as setting forth the space planning requirements.

Compact Shelving

The primary motive for the development of compact shelving over the past few decades has been to provide a better way to utilize existing space because the cost of new construction has risen so dramatically. Compact shelving eliminates the non-productive aisles required for stationery shelving by mounting shelves on mobile bases or "dollies." The dollies are equipped with ball bearing assemblies so they can move heavy weight loads with relatively little effort on the part of the user.

The mobile units usually roll on premounted tracks. The tracks are laid on top of an existing floor and leveled. In construction of a new facility, specialized application tracks can be recessed directly into the floor.

The mobile units are placed in rows, one in front of the other with only a few inches of clearance space between rows. Such a configuration can increase existing storage space from 30 to 100 percent, the degree of gain depending upon how compact the arrangement is made.

Three modes of compact shelving are available: manual, mechanical assist, and electrical. Small systems usually rely on manual or mechanical assist to move the ranges. Large systems are usually electrical. Manual systems are not recommended for ranges longer than 15 feet even though the force required to move a range is less than one-half of one percent of the weight to be moved. That is because a fully loaded range of 15 feet weighs approximately 7,500 pounds. Mechanically assisted systems can handle ranges up to 30 feet in length and require a force less than one-twentieth of the weight to be moved. Electrical systems can be used with ranges up to 60 feet in length.

Safety devices are installed in these systems to prevent aisles from being inadvertently closed. Floor safety sweeps run the full length of the range and will stop the movement of the range when activated by a force of two pounds. Pressure-sensitive safety sweeps run the length of each range at waist height. A force of less than one pound against the sweep will stop range movement. Finally, most vendors put a series of tape switches in the floor at intervals. Fifty pounds of pressure will activate the switches and stop the ranges from moving.

All three types of systems are easy to use—most are operated by a single handle or switch.

The highest percentage of gain will be in an area of lowest activity since more mobile rows and larger mobile units can be used. The difficulty comes in trying to use this type of storage in an area that contains heavily used materials. If it is likely that a number of patrons would seek access to the material at any one time, it is not realistic to provide only one open aisle.

In installations accommodating fewer than 10,000 volumes only one access point is provided, with different rows moving into and out of access position. For larger installations two or more access points are provided. The degree of activity, the number of people to be given access, and the size of the storage area are all considerations that must be taken into account when determining the number of access points.

There are a number of suppliers of compact shelving systems, among them Lundia, Spacesaver, and White.

Compact Filing

Compact filing systems usually have much smaller storage capacities than compact shelving systems. The vertical carousel rotates to deliver records, pamphlets, or even books to the operator workstation. Computer control can be added to speed retrieval. While a compact shelving system can be designed to accommodate multiple users, compact filing systems assume a single user, usually a full-time file clerk.

The major supplier of compact filing systems is Kardex. The product is called the Lektriever.

Compact filing systems are extremely efficient in terms of the number of pieces or volumes stored per square foot. The cost per piece or volume housed, however, is higher than the costs of compact shelving systems. The breakdown rate is also greater.

Some units have to be on the ground floor because they require a floor capable of accommodating a load of 420 pounds per square foot. Not even all ground floors have this floor loading capacity. Lektriever requires approximately 170 pounds per square foot and can be put on almost any floor if the equipment is spaced properly. The greatest drawback of these systems is that they require staff operation. They are "closed access systems." Libraries have tended to prefer "open access systems," which let users retrieve their own materials and do not require that materials be rearranged from their regular shelving sequence.

A discussion of the two types is essential at this point.

Closed Access Systems

A closed access system is one that would only be available to a limited number of staff. The material is brought to the operator. While Kardex's Lektriever is an example, the older Randtriever is a more suitable illustration for librarians. While not a carousel design, the concept is very similar.

In the Randtriever—which was initially developed as a filing system—books are stored in boxes 8" wide, 12" high, and 15" deep containing an average of 12.5 volumes per box. Boxes are kept on shelves with the 8" side facing the aisle. The shelves are 5'8" long. The shelves are carried by uprights, providing double-faced ranges. The ranges are spaced 4'4" apart, center to center.

The books are placed in the boxes in a fixed location order with each box having its own machine-readable code number, which is recorded in the computerized control at the console.

Between each two ranges an upright post moves back and forth on tracks attached to the floor and ceiling. On each post is a mechanized picker that moves to the end of the range and places the box on a conveyor belt that delivers it to the computer console, where the electronic control verifies the correctness of the transaction. An operator takes the appropriate book from the box, charges it out to the borrower, gives the book to the patron, and sends the box back to the shelves. This procedure is reversed when the book is returned. A variant on the Randtriever is the Lektriever, which moves the shelves to the operator's position in a ferris-wheel-like action.

A patron wishing to get a book from Randtriever looks up its control number in the catalog and gives the number to the operator who punches it into the computer. If the book has already been charged out, the computer tells the operator before he searches the shelves. The average time for retrieving a box from the shelves is 23 seconds. A slightly longer time is required to return the box to the shelves.

In addition to requiring staffing, the Randtriever also is handicapped by the fact that it exerts a pressure of 420 pounds per square foot. Few libraries can accommodate such floor loads except when the space has been specifically constructed for this type of storage system.

Open Access Systems

The compact shelving systems sold by Lundia, Spacesaver, and White are "open access systems." This refers to the design, not their actual use. They have been used in a number of libraries and information centers both in closed access areas and in areas that are open to the public. The majority of smaller installations are open access. The large installations, in academic and public libraries are often not open to the public; not because they couldn't be, but because the libraries have a tradition of closed stacks for parts of their collections.

Floor Loading

As popular as compact shelving systems have become, they have their drawbacks. A typical system is very heavy and not suitable for some areas of a building. Typically, compact shelving requires a load-bearing floor capable of accommodating 180 to 200 pounds per square foot, although by reducing the storage capacity to 6 shelves per section or by using special weight distribution techniques the requirement can be reduced to 150 pounds per square foot—the most common load-bearing capacity in libraries and information centers designed for conventional library shelving. The floor loading should be checked carefully by an engineer or against available structural engineering documents before such shelving systems are installed.

When the floor loading permits it, stacks should be placed on 4'4" centers, thus providing a 30" aisle. This is enough for persons to pass one another with comfort and for standard lighting to reach the bottom shelves.

InterRoyal, best known for warehouse storage systems, makes a high-rise compact shelving system. Instead of moving the aisles conventional shelving is built to heights of 30 feet and pages move up and down and along the shelves on special electromechanical platforms. This type of system is practical only in special storage warehouses such as those built by several academic libraries.

Lighting

If each potential aisle has a separate light control, operating costs can be reduced. Overhead lighting can be synchronized with the opening and closing of aisles, providing lighting to accessed areas only. If the lights for an entire area are on a single switch, lighting strips should be run perpendicular to the stacks so that the light level will be uniform throughout the stacks.

Cost

Cost is an important factor in planning to use compact storage. The cost is normally justified only to avoid new construction or remodeling that would cost in excess of $80 per square foot. The cost of compact shelving may be nearly three times as great as conventional library/information center shelving. The cost can be reduced by selecting a system that can use the shelving components of the conventional library shelving which the organization already has.

Questions

The following questions should be answered when thinking about the possibility of compact storage:

a. Is there sufficient space to maintain the rate of growth of materials and, if there is, for how long?
b. How will the cost of compact storage compare with the cost of conventional shelving?
c. Can existing shelving and file equipment be readily converted to a compact storage system or must it be replaced? If the latter is the case, what trade-in value is obtainable and what would be the cost of replacement?
d. Is the estimated weight of the compact storage system compatible with the weight load capabilities of the floor on which it is installed?
e. If the floor must be reinforced, what will be involved and how much will it cost?
f. Is the prospective compact storage layout compatible with the activity and flow of records to and from the storage area?

Summary

There are now hundreds of installations of compact storage—primarily compact shelving—most of them in special libraries and corporate information centers. Many libraries provide their patrons access to the storage areas. In the past five years the Lektriever, Randtriever, and variants of them have fallen into disfavor because they do not provide for direct patron access and because the cost is higher than for compact shelving systems such as Spacesaver, which costs approximately $300 per three-foot double-faced section.

The most appropriate uses for compact shelving are the areas of the collection that are not heavily used: special collections, government documents, backfiles of journals, etc.

Floor loading should be determined before undertaking a detailed investigation of the technology. Anything less than 150 pounds per square foot is inadequate. Floor loading in excess of 170 pounds is preferred, and floor loading of more than 200 pounds is ideal.

Space Requirements

The formulas in Chapter 8 should be used to determine space requirements, with adjustments made for the elimination of the aisles. Special libraries should adjust the figures for book storage because of the relative thickness of their bound volumes. If there are no floor loading or heavy traffic constraints, the capacities can be doubled when replacing conventional shelving with compact storage.

8

EXISTING SPACE PLANNING FORMULAS

The formulas currently used by library and information center planners usually include provision for reading space, stack space, and service space. It is normally assumed that most seating will be at four-place tables, with each person requiring no more than 25 square feet for working space and adjacent circulation space. This means a table surface area of 6 square feet per person. It is assumed that in a special library/information center environment no more than 5 percent of the users will need to be accommodated at any one time; and that patterns of past use can be the basis for seating an even smaller percentage. The figure for public libraries is usually .5 percent. The figure for academic libraries is usually 25 percent of the users; with academic law libraries requiring 50 percent.

Those conducting research are assumed to require more space, normally in carrells (individual tables which have visual barriers on three sides). These carrells and the adjacent circulation space are estimated to take 30 square feet each.

The formulas generally provide for the storage of 10 bound volumes per square foot of floor space. The calculations are based on storing materials on standard library shelving that is set up in ranges which are 4'4" apart at their centers. This provides aisles of 30 to 36 inches in width, depending upon the depth of the shelves. This would result in shelves that are approximately 75 percent full, slightly more than the optimum 67 percent figure recommended by many planners, but below the 86 percent at which shelves reach maximum working capacity. A capacity greater than 86 percent results in the constant shifting of volumes as new materials are added.

Public libraries often seek to accommodate 15 books per square foot by planning for shelves which are nearly full when all books are in. The high level of circulation and regular weeding common in most public libraries make it possible to use this figure. Law libraries, on the other hand, must plan seven books per square foot because the average book is considerably thicker than in other types of libraries. The formulas require just minor modification to accommodate these different types of libraries.

Materials other than bound volumes are usually converted to volume equivalents as follows:

Type of Holding	Vol. Equiv. Fact.
Bound volumes	1.00
Maps (each sheet)	0.30
Government Documents (linear feet)	6.00
Archives Materials (linear feet)	6.00
Optical and Phono Disks (linear feet)	6.00
Films, 16mm and 8mm (reels)	1.00
Video Tapes (cartridges)	1.00
Audio Tapes and Cassettes	0.25
Film Strips	0.25
Microfilms (reels)	0.25
Microfiche and Cards (each piece)	0.01

Space for library staff is provided for as a percentage of the total amount of study and stacks space in the library or information center. Commonly 5 percent of the total space generated for table, carrell, and stack space is allotted for library or information center service, including both those who serve the public and those who acquire and process materials. Some formulas specifically provide for a minimum number of square feet per staff member. The most common is 150 square feet per staff member.

Summary of Formulas Used for Library Space Planning

The following formulas—almost all of them developed by state higher education planning bodies—are in general use:

CALIFORNIA STATE UNIVERSITY AND COLLEGES (CSUC) SPACE FORMULA

The CSUC formula calls for 25 square feet for library reader stations and 35 square feet for special reader stations that contain typewriters, computer terminals, facilities for the physically handicapped, etc.

The reader space standards require that 90 percent of the reader stations be projected at 25 square feet per station and 10 percent be designated for special functions at 35 square feet per station.

The library stack area section of the formula calls for one square foot per 10 volumes for the active portion of the collection; one square foot per linear foot for projected government publications; 25 percent of the total calculated active volume allocation and government publications allocation for nonvolume type materials (films, video tapes, maps, etc.); and one square foot per 30 volumes for projected inactive volumes.

Staff space standards are set at 225 square feet per projected FTE staff position.

ILLINOIS UNIVERSITY LIBRARY SPACE FORMULA

The Illinois University Space Formula assumes that the space required is planned so that each shelf is filled to about 75 percent capacity. The space for the stack collections is 0.1 square foot per bound volume; or 1 square foot per 10 bound volumes. As total collection size increases, however, the need for stack area decreases and shelves holding some of the least used books can be filled to greater capacity. The recommended standards for stack space are:

First 150,000 volumes	.1 square foot per bound vol.
Next 150,000 volumes	.09 square foot per bound vol.
Next 300,000 volumes	.08 square foot per bound vol.

Certain materials other than books also require stack space. The recommended space for these materials on a conversion basis is shown below:

Item	Unit	Conversion Factor
Pamphlets, documents	Item	10.0
Serials	Item	1.0
Newspapers	Item	0.07
Microfilm	Reel	3.5
Microfiche, Microprint	Card	77.0
Maps	Item	7.0
Slides	Item	20.0
Recordings	Item	5.0
Unprocessed material	Volume	1.0

The following standards are recommended for reading room space: 7.5 square feet per user potentially to be served and 15 square feet per researcher.

Library service space includes both technical and public services areas. This space is based on a percentage of reader space with the value of 25 percent being used. Where branch libraries are to be constructed, only 20 percent of the reader space should be allowed for service space within the branch library, the remaining 5 percent to be allowed in the main library for activities connected with centralized acquisitions and cataloging.

GUIDELINES FOR ASSESSING THE ADEQUACY OF ACADEMIC LIBRARIES IN NEW YORK STATE

In developing minimal quantitative guidelines, New York state relies heavily on the Clapp-Jordan Formula, developed in 1965. Volume is used as a basic measure for counting. One "unit" of library resources is:

a. one volume
b. one reel of microfilm
c. eight microcards
d. four sheets of microprint
e. one-seventh sheet of ultrafiche

f. eight sheets of microfiche
g. forty 35mm slides or one bibliographically described slide set
h. one multimedia kit or set

The formula allows for variables among institutions with respect to academic programs and institutional size. When applied to an individual institution's program, they serve as a model for threshold adequacy constructed in minimum terms and afford a basis for long-range developmental planning.

The formula for the library's space requirements has three components:

Seating Factor   The library seating factor, based upon the number of users to be served, depends on the type of library. A research facility requires more space than a community college. The recommended factor for a research library is 7.25 square feet for each potential user.

Collection Factor   Collection factors depend in part upon the overall size of the collection. Space requirements for collections should be calculated by using the following collection factors cumulatively as needed. To arrive at the number of volumes use either the formula determination of units of resources required or the actual calculation of units held before application of any bonus credits, whichever is greater.

Number of Volumes	Square Feet/Volume
First 150,000 volumes	0.10
Next 150,000 volumes	0.09

Several cautions should be observed in utilizing these guidelines:

- They apply to conventional library services only. If the library building houses audiovisual services, classrooms, language labs, or other such activities, space for them should be added to the totals developed through the use of these guidelines.
- Although centralization or decentralization of library services in an institution may have considerable impact

upon library staffing requirements, it exerts little if any influence upon the total amount of library space required.

- All conventional library activities, whether specifically mentioned in these guidelines or not, are incorporated somewhere within them.
- Use of these guidelines produces spatial estimates in terms of net assignable square feet only; gross square footages may be determined by adding appropriate net-to-gross increments to them.

Administrative Factor The Administrative factor accounts for space required for such administrative activities as processing a collection (including acquisitions, cataloging, and binding), serving the public (including service desks, catalogs, and special files), and library management functions (including requisite staff areas).

This administrative factor may be calculated at 25 percent of the square feet required for seating and collections as determined under the first two factors.

WESTERN INTERSTATE COMMISSION FOR HIGHER EDUCATION. PLANNING AND MANAGEMENT SYSTEMS DIVISION. MANUAL FOUR: ACADEMIC SUPPORT FACILITIES

This approach differs from that of the formulas previously mentioned because as a consortium WICHE serves its members solely as a source of information that they may use in developing their own formulas. In addressing the question of using any measure of volumes per assignable square foot, WICHE points out that the degree to which stack shelving can be packed without incurring operational inefficiencies is a matter of debate. If collections are densely packed, new acquisitions cannot be added in call number sequence without frequent and costly reshelving. WICHE notes that many states have adopted a planning factor of 0.0833 Assignable Square Foot per volume (12 volumes per ASF) as a guideline. In some instances, a factor of 0.10 Assignable Square Foot, or 10 volumes per ASF is used. Generally, the factor includes an allowance for either unbound materials and other items not included in the counted "volumes."

The formula examines the attention that has been given to compact storage of little used but still valuable library materials. Off-site compact storage in lower cost facilities has its attractions. WICHE notes the evidence that the costs of off-site compact storage are greater than the savings of capital investment which is required to expand normal, central stack storage. The operating costs of selecting, removing, recataloging, transporting, retrieving, and returning the materials should be carefully considered before a major move toward remote compact storage is attempted. WICHE also observes that some delays in construction of new library facilities force compact storage irrespective of operating costs.

In developing detailed evaluation and projection of reader station requirements, an in-depth analysis of the library user population is called for. In the absence of such a study, WICHE recommends a maximum of 25 square feet per reader for up to one-fourth of the population to be served, with more space provided if equipment is to be included at the reader stations.

WICHE is most definitive with regard to staffing requirements, specifying a minimum of 150 square feet per staff member unless special equipment is to be provided near the staff desks.

MARYLAND COUNCIL FOR HIGHER EDUCATION. HIGHER EDUCATION SPACE UTILIZATION STANDARDS MANUAL: MANUAL II

The section of this manual dealing with library space planning begins with rather general definitions and moves to specific worksheets for calculating space requirements. An interesting assumption in this document is that "a library is a unique facility that when properly designed can serve efficiently for 50 to 100 years."

Seating should be provided for 5 to 15 percent of potential users at no less than 25 square feet per reader. More space is recommended for special functions such as the use of microform, audio-visual, or other equipment.

Required study stations are allocated on the following formula:

Tables for 4 or more—not more than 20%
Lounge chairs—no more than 10%
Individual Seating Facilities—up to 85%

Total stack requirements are computed by converting library materials to the Bound Volume Equivalents from the following conversion table.

Type of Holding	Unit	BVE
Bound volumes	volume	1.00
Documents and pamphlets	item	0.10
Microfilm reels	reel	0.30
Newspapers—unbound	item	14.30
Newspapers—bound	volume	14.30
Periodicals—unbound	item	1.00
Periodicals—bound	volume	1.00
Records (recording)	recording	0.20

The overall space requirement is determined as follows:

First 150,000 BVE   .10 NASF
Second 150,000 BVE   .09 NASF

The volume capacity per stack section is assumed to be 147 volumes (7 volumes per linear foot of shelf), but some empty shelf space is required for operational manipulation. Eighty-six percent of the actual shelf capacity is recognized as a maximum operation level. A value of 100 volumes per stack section for open access libraries under 50,000 BVE and 120 volumes per stack section of those of 100,000 BVE or more are considered good operating norms.

Stacks open to patrons should have 36" aisles and generous cross-walks. Consequently, stack space for the general collection should be calculated at 8 NASF per stack. This is the most generous of any formula.

The Maryland Formula goes into considerable detail about space requirements for public service duty stations and technical processing work areas. Generally, the requirement is a minimum of 150 square feet per staff member.

Converting Linear to Square Feet

Many librarians are accustomed to calculating their library shelving requirements in linear feet. Architects tend to think in terms of square feet. To convert linear feet to square feet using a module of space:

- Measure the distance between columns. Multiply length by width to determine square feet enclosed. If the distances between all columns are the same, the square foot area between each column will make up one bay or module of space. If the space enclosed by four columns is 20 feet by 20 feet, one module contains 400 square feet.
- Lay out book stacks by marking out the center pole of one double-faced range to the center pole of the next. If a 36-inch aisle is desired and the shelves are 12 inches deep, the space to be spanned from one center pole to the next will be 5 feet.
- Count the number of book stacks one can lay out in the space. In a module of 400 square feet, there are normally 24 double-faced stacks.
- Count the number of single-faced stacks. In a module of 400 square feet, there are normally 48 single-faced stacks.
- Determine the linear feet of shelving in each section. If all stacks are 3 feet wide and 7 shelves high, each single face contains 21 linear feet.
- Multiply the number of linear feet in one single-faced section by the number of sections. In our example, there are 21 linear feet × 48 single-faced sections, which equals 1,008 linear feet.
- Determine the number of volumes per linear foot (using standards or random sampling of shelves). In our example, there are 7 volumes per linear foot; 1,008 × 7 = 7,056 volumes in the collection in that module or bay.

- Divide the number of volumes by the square feet in the module.

7,056 volumes

400 square feet = 17.64 volumes per square foot

Reliance on Formulas

While the practice of requiring quantitative formulas is generally limited to academic institutions, librarians and building consultants regularly use the available formulas in planning all types of libraries, making the adjustments previously mentioned.

Rather than adopting a formula developed for academic libraries, there is an informal formula which public libraries may wish to consider. It calls for making a 20-year projection of population growth and providing 1 square foot per person. Alternatively, the 20-year population projection can be used to calculate the book storage requirement and the number of reader seats. Book requirements are estimated at the rate of four per capita—except in communities of over 150,000 for which two per capita is more common—with one square foot provided for each 15 books. Readers seats are estimated at the rate of five seats per 1,000 people, with 25 square feet per seat. Staff space is estimated at 15 percent of the total building area. In addition, space would have to be added for meeting rooms and other special facilities.

Special libraries should also be careful in using the formulas described in this chapter. They may have much thicker volumes. For example, law and medical libraries can accommodate only seven volumes per square foot. Most special libraries will also need to accommodate a larger percentage of the potential users at any one time. For example, 50 percent is a common figure for academic law libraries. The professional literature should be consulted for specific criteria for each type of special library.

Formula Revisions Required

The existing formulas are deficient in several respects: they do not provide sufficient reader space when equipment is required to access information; they fail to provide for the use of compact storage; microform is considered only in terms of storage requirements; and no provision is made for the use of optical media and digital telefacsimile. It is, therefore, necessary to use these formulas with caution and to seek to modify them to meet the changing requirements. That is the focus of the next chapter.

9
Space Planning Recommendations

While it would be short-sighted to plan a library or information center using hard-copy-oriented planning formulas without modification, it is premature to base plans on the concept of the "paperless" library or information center. The vast majority of recorded information is available only in printed form: books, journals, government documents, maps, etc.

A library or information center that is committed to making maximum use of information available in electronic form will find that only bibliographic information is widely available and that much of it is available only on large computer systems at remote locations. Access to these remotely housed data bases requires only a terminal and modem. Few organizations have yet adopted the concept of micro-based workstations capable of accessing all appropriate computer resources, whether remote or locally stored on mass storage media.

Converting eye-readable information available locally into machine-readable form using optical scanning equipment is still labor intensive and costly. Loading commercially available magnetic tapes of machine-readable data bases into the storage now available on local systems is not cost effective. Full-text information is still rarely available in electronic format.

While it is generally believed that optical mass storage media such as digitally encoded videodiscs, optical digital disks, and CD-ROM will facilitate electronic publishing and the mounting of very large bibliographic and full-text data bases on local systems, it takes several years for that which is technologically feasible to become widely available. The factors that constrain the diffusion of a new technology include technological, economic, legal, and attitudinal forces.

Despite the fact that there are now a number of digital videodisc, optical digital disk, and CD-ROM based systems available, the technologies are not yet widely used. This is in large part due to the fact that major production investments are awaiting the completion of relevant standards. Another technological constraint is the lack of reliable, high-speed optical character recognition devices for converting eye-readable information to digital form. The fact that there are fewer than ten disk pressing plants worldwide is also inhibiting development.

The lack of mass-produced systems has kept prices high. To date only relatively small bibliographic data bases (under 2/5 billion characters) can be made available on CD-ROM as cost effectively as online.

Copyright is also a factor. Those who hold the copyright on printed materials are often reluctant to license electronic publication because they know little of the technology and fear that they will lose control over distribution and use.

Attitudinal factors include not only the attitudes of librarians and information specialists, but also of users and potential publishers of information. Librarians and information specialists fear that users will resist the new media as they have resisted microform in the past. Potential publishers often have a strong, even irrational commitment to the print medium. Manufacturers of the hardware tend to focus their efforts on the markets that appear to have the greatest potential. The library and information center markets have generally been ignored.

Because of the slow diffusion of new information technologies, it is necessary to plan new library and information center facilities to accommodate print, video, and electronic formats; and to provide for only a gradual augmentation and limited displacement of print by other media.

For all of the above reasons, library and information space planning has not changed a great deal in the past 30 years. The primary emphasis has been on providing space for printed or written materials, readers, and staff. Formulas have been adopted to facilitate the determination of space requirements and existing libraries and information centers have been studied for ideas about layout, furnishings, and finishes.

The facilities being planned now must accommodate all of these technologies because they will become viable during the useful life of any facility constructed during the latter half of the eighties. A number of the information technologies affect design requirements. For example, library automation is no longer confined to the technical services area or the circulation desk; patron access terminals may have to be accommodated throughout the building. Any carrell could potentially include a personal micro or a terminal. The reference department may soon be receiving electronic publications on CD-ROM or digitally encoded videodiscs. Electronic document delivery may also be widely used. Information centers will probably have to accommodate micro-based workstations with peripheral mass storage devices containing large data bases on most staff desks and at many user desks.

The response to these emerging requirements is to stress flexibility, but maximizing flexibility may significantly increase costs. Building for the future is a particular problem when the formulae by which space requirements and budgets are determined have not been adjusted to allow for the emerging technologies. This chapter, therefore, emphasizes the need to retain expert advice and the minimum provisions architects should be asked to make in designing library or information center facilities:

1. *Retain qualified architects and consultants when planning facilities.*

The complexity of space planning in a changing environment makes it more important than ever that librarians and information specialists retain the services of qualified architects and consultants. The former should have experience with libraries and information centers, and the latter should be an expert in the information technologies which the facility is to accommodate and in library/information center services. An architect should be retained for any project over $10,000 that involves partitioning, electrical, air conditioning, or other major systems. A consultant should be retained for any project over $50,000 or one which is intended to meet the needs of the library or information center for a period of at least five years: the period of time within which information technologies will affect virtually all institutions.

An architect's services typically comprise the following:
- analysis of the client's requirements, including planning, programming, and research;
- preliminary design drawings;
- preparation of preliminary cost estimates;
- final design drawings and updating of cost estimates;
- working drawings and specifications suitable for a builder to carry out construction;
- preparation of bidding or tender period;
- administration of the bidding or tender period;
- advice to the client on selection of a suitable contractor;
- supervision of the construction process;
- incorporating changes as may be necessary during the construction period;
- checking of contractor's claims for payment;
- final inspection of the building; and
- certifying final payments.

A consultant's role is usually to:
- evaluate existing library facilities and operations;
- recommend changes in the library facilities and operations relative to the new building, especially insofar as new information technologies affect planning;
- participate in the planning process, and assist in the definition of a philosophy of library service with respect to the collection, readers and staff, as well as suggesting sizing standards for these;
- assist in the preparation of the written architectural program statement;
- review preliminary and final plans;
- advise on selection and layout of library furnishings, especially with a view toward incorporating information technologies into them.

2. *Include a computer room and provide for installation of terminals when constructing facilities.*
A large majority of libraries and information centers can be expected to be automated by 1995. All new construction or

major remodeling should, therefore, include a computer room. Libraries with collections of more than 100,000 volumes should anticipate the installation of a minicomputer-based system and should use the generic site preparation requirements set forth in Chapter 3. Smaller libraries and information centers should scale down the requirements as noted. Very large libraries that plan to install more than 100 terminals should enlarge the room by 50 percent for each 100 additional terminals.

Provision should be made for terminals and micro-based workstations to be located throughout the library(ies). There should be space above the ceiling for pulling shielded data transmission cable of up to 3/4 inch in diameter. All finished columns should include a blank duct with an inside diameter of at least 1 inch for the pulling of data transmission cable from the ceiling, thus avoiding "power poles" as much as possible. Data transmission cabling from columns to terminals or micro-based workstations should be accomplished by placing furniture close to columns to permit concealment of wiring or by using flat cable under the carpeting.

Staff desks should be provided with dedicated electrical outlets for micro-based workstations as well as with regular electrical outlets. The dedicated circuit protects the sensitive micros from interference from typewriters and other devices with motors.

3. *Space for the storage of printed materials on conventional shelving should continue to be based on the 10 volumes per square foot formula, adjusted to 20 volumes per square foot when compact storage is used.*

The formula of 10 volumes per square foot is widely used and should continue to be used. The formula should be doubled to 20 volumes per square foot when compact storage is used. Compact storage is usually cost effective when the cost of construction is in excess of $80 per square foot. Materials other than bound volumes should be converted to volume equivalents using one of the formulas presented in Chapter 8.

The formula should be doubled when planning compact storage. An open access system, such as Spacesaver, is preferable over limited access compact storage because it does not require staff intervention to retrieve materials, is less expensive, less heavy, and more reliable. Existing shelving can be incorporated into the new system to further reduce the cost. Depending on the equipment selected, compact storage can more than double the storage capacity of an area. A figure of 20 volumes per square foot is recommended, however, because it will be valid for any one of several systems that may be selected. Any compact storage system that cannot accommodate at least 20 volumes per square foot should not be considered unless additional space is available only at extraordinary cost.

Libraries and information centers should make sure that as space requirements are reduced by using compact storage, a proportion of the money saved in reducing the size of the facility is made available for the purchase of the storage equipment. Academic libraries in particular have often found that they have been required to purchase the relatively expensive storage equipment with furniture and equipment budgets which have not been adjusted to reflect a change in approach. The best way to avoid this problem is to include the compact equipment in the architectural contract so that the architect incorporates it as part of the facilities plan and contractors bid the equipment as a building component.

4. *Floor loading should be a minimum of 150 pounds per square foot, with 200 pounds in areas planned for compact or microform storage.*

The single most important factor modifying the proper allocation of space in a library or information center is the ability of the floor to bear the weight of stacks and equipment. The ability of any structure to bear weight can be stated in terms of "dead load" and "live load." The former is the weight of the structure itself. The latter consists of the elements that can be moved around the building.

Conventional library shelving consisting of seven shelves per section and spaced on 4'4" centers to create 30–36 inch aisles requires a "live load" or floor loading of 150 pounds. This means that the weight of objects such as the stacks, books, etc. should not exceed 150 pounds per square foot averaged across the floor. This does not mean that in a specific square foot the weight may not exceed 150 pounds. Most office buildings can handle only 75 pounds per square foot. Special libraries accommodated in office buildings, therefore, should be particularly careful to obtain information about their areas.

Ideally, areas in which compact storage or microform

storage equipment is to be located should have a floor loading of 200 pounds. This provides for seven shelves per section and an aisle of just 30 inches in the case of the former; and 11 drawer filing cabinets in the case of the latter. If the floor loading is reduced to 170 pounds the number of shelves has to be reduced to six and the number of drawers to nine.

5. *Microform areas should be planned for limited growth, but with attention to the standards of applied micrographics.*

Microform is cost effective only when it is used in lieu of binding. The pay-back period for converting hard copy to microform is usually too long to justify its use. A library should, therefore, be judicious in its use of microform as a space saving technique.

Microform may be displayed by optical media. The change may take several years, however, and it is unlikely that a library will be able to convert its microform holdings to optical media. The new media will probably augment rather than displace the older medium. Microform facilities will, therefore, remain part of almost all libraries.

Care should be taken to plan the facilities in a manner consistent with the standards of applied micrographics set forth in Chapter 5. There should be not only emphasis on proper storage equipment and reading areas with a minimum of 35 square feet per person, but also on environmental factors such as humidity control and low glare.

6. *Patron seating in carrells should be calculated at 35 square feet per person.*

The widely adopted standard of 25 square feet per person has been recognized as inadequate when computer or audio-visual equipment is included in a carrell (an individual reading table with visual barriers). Few formulas, however, provide for more square footage. Only the formula of the California State Colleges and University provide for 35 square feet per carrell, but it limits the number of such carrells to 10 percent of the total.

Most facilities that provide larger carrells for microform, micro-based work stations, audio-visual, personal computer, or other electronic equipment have had to reduce the total number of carrells so that a small percentage can be oversize. The prospect that electronic equipment will be widely used in the future makes it imperative that the formula of 35 square feet be adopted for all carrells throughout a facility to accommodate carrells of at least 42 by 30 inches and sufficient circulating space.

If it is not possible to install carrells suitable for electronic equipment throughout a library, provision should be made for a minimum percentage to be oversize. In light of the future potential of micro-based workstations and optical media the lowest acceptable percentage for an academic, school, or special library is 25 percent. A public library should seek a minimum of 10 percent. All of the carrells in the reference area should be oversize, however, as should all units in microform and media areas.

Regular table seating should be limited to two and four place tables, with each person having a minimum of 24 by 36 inches of workspace. A minimum of 25 square feet per person should be planned for individual table seating and the associated circulating space.

7. Work areas should be a minimum of 175 square feet per staff member.

Existing formulas recognize that staff in libraries and information centers work with materials and must have more space than regular office workers. A minimum of 150 square feet is well established, although some formulas provide as much as 225 square feet. With the advent of information technologies, larger desks are needed (30 by 72 inches) and additional console equipment such as CAR and optical media devices may be installed. A minimum of 175 square feet should be adopted. It may be necessary to increase this figure to 200 square feet in situations in which staff work with a CAR system with a capacity of more than 1 million pages (frames), or with a videodisc-based system.

Professional staff should have individual offices of approximately 200 square feet each to accommodate oversized work surfaces, materials on "trucks," and individual training. If this much space cannot be assigned, space should be provided immediately outside each office for vertical files, "truck" storage, etc.

Support staff should have desks separated by office landscape equipment. The areas should provide at least 175 square feet per person because staff have to process materials and use electronic equipment. If this much space cannot be provided—

a situation that is most often encountered in special library situations because the parent organization often has inflexible formulas that tie the size of an office to the paygrade of a worker—a common area should be provided for vertical files, "truck" storage, and the like.

All staff desks should be a minimum of 30 by 72 inches to provide space for a micro-based workstation consisting of a personal computer with screen and keyboard, CD-ROM or other mass storage device, and noiseless printer.

Each staff desk should have a telephone outlet and a two socket 110 volt electrical outlet for typewriters, computer printers, etc. A color-coded, two-socket 110 volt electrical outlet should be provided at each staff desk for a computer terminal or micro-based workstation and associated data storage. These outlets should not be on the same circuit as typewriters, computer printers, or any other equipment that has a motor.

8. *Full-height partitions should be kept to a minimum in the staff areas.*

The work space should be highly flexible. Only professional offices and work areas that are noisy—electronics repair, binding and mending, microfilming, etc.—should be fully enclosed. Office landscape should be used extensively. The use of office landscape will require the introduction of "white noise" to minimize distractions. Provision should be made for "tuning" the system after the facility is occupied.

9. *No specially constructed desks or carrells should be planned.*

All desks and carrells in staff and patron areas should be so designed that a cable 1/4 inch in diameter can be concealed inside a hollow leg and/or behind an apron. Specially constructed furniture should be avoided, not only because it is more expensive initially, but also because it is extremely costly to buy additional or replacement units later when quantity discounts do not apply. Standard furniture can accommodate electrical and data cable if care is taken to select equipment which can conceal the cabling.

It is also important that the furniture selected meet the ergonomic requirements of electronic equipment. Table and chair heights are more critical when using keyboards and screens than when reading books. Tables and carrells should not exceed 28 inches in height and chairs should be in proportion to the work surfaces.

10. *Provision should be made for digital telefacsimile equipment.*

The interlibrary loan area or another suitable area in the library should be planned to accommodate a digital telefacsimile device. The space requirement does not exceed 35 square feet, but there should be a dedicated 15 AMP electrical outlet, a telephone outlet, and proximity to a photocopier which can be used to photocopy bound materials.

11. *Special provision should be made to minimize static electricity.*

Because of the large amount of electronic equipment that libraries and information centers will have to accommodate in the future it is important that special care be taken to minimize static electricity.

There should be no carpeting in the computer room. The floor should not require waxing. All carpeting in technical services and other staff areas should be antistatic, as should that in reference, microform, and media areas—the public areas that will have the greatest concentration of electronic equipment. All electronic equipment should be grounded. Antistatic chair mats that can be grounded should be used in front of other electronic equipment: digital telefacsimile machines, patron access catalog terminals in other areas of the facility, and other appropriate equipment. Static buildup is more common when people are moving their feet.

12. *Special attention should be paid to minimizing glare.*

All lighting throughout the facility should be indirect, recessed, or parabolic so that glare on computer terminal or micro workstation screens, video screens, and microform reader screens will not be a problem. No desks or carrells should be positioned where direct sunlight can reflect off equipment screens.

The emphasis in planning lighting should be on the quality of light, rather than the level of light. Any screen is easy to read in a lighted room if there is no glare. Special lighting for areas with electronic equipment should, therefore, be avoided.

13. *Dry pipe sprinkling systems should be used to minimize water damage.*

Sprinkling systems are required in many jurisdictions. These present a threat to books and other library materials when they go off accidentally, or as the result of vandalism. While it is now possible to salvage most water damaged printed materials using freeze drying techniques, water can cause irreparable damage to electronic equipment. It is, therefore, highly desirable to specify that there be no water in the pipes and that the system be zoned. In such a dry-pipe system, water is released into the appropriate zone of the system only when a fire hazard has been detected.

Finally, the best preparation for facilities planning is for librarians and informations specialists to become and remain technology literate. All of the technologies mentioned in this book will be significant throughout the next decade.

BIBLIOGRAPHY

Ad Hoc Committee on the Physical Facilities of Libraries. *Measurement and Comparison of the Physical Facilities for Libraries.* Chicago: Library Administration Division, American Library Assn., 1970.

American Institute of Architects. *The Library Building.* Building Type Reference Guide, no. 3. Chicago: American Library Assn., 1947.

American Library Association Standards Committee. *Minimum Standards for Public Library Systems, 1966.* Chicago: American Library Assn., 1967.

"Are Microforms an Answer/Partial Answer to Library Space Problems?" In *Running out of Space—What Are the Alternatives?* Edited by Gloria Novak. Chicago: American Library Assn., 1978.

Asleson, Robert F. "Microforms as an alternative to Building." In *Running out ot Space—What Are the Alternatives?* Edited by Gloria Novak. Chicago: American Library Assn., 1978.

Beckman, Margaret. "Problems of Library Facilities in Research Environments." *Journal of Society of Research Administrators* 12 (summer 1980):11–15.

Bloss, Meredith. "Field/Performance Theory Applied to Library Space Planning." *Library Journal Special Report #1: Library Space Planning,* 1976.

Boca Basic Building Code, 1981. 8th ed. Chicago: Building Officials and Code Administrators International, 1981.

Boll, John J. "To Grow or Not to Grow? A Review of Alternatives to New Academic Library Buildings." *Library Journal Special Report #15.* New York: R. R. Bowker, 1980.

Boss, Richard W., and Deborah Raikes. *Developing Microform Reading Facilities.* Westport, Conn.: Microform Review, 1981.

Cassata, Mary B. "Book Storage." *Library Trends,* January 1971.

Cohen, Aaron, and Elaine Cohen. *Designing and Space Planning for Libraries: A Behavioral Guide.* New York: R. R. Bowker, 1979.

Cohen, Aaron, and Elaine Cohen. "Do Our Library Buildings Have to Be Discarded Every Fifteen Years." *Library Journal Special Report #1: Library Space Planning,* 1976.

Cohen, Aaron, and Elaine Cohen. Letter to the editor commenting on Lawrence Lieberfeld's article and a response from Lieberfeld. *College and Research Libraries* 45 (January 1984):71–72.

Cohen, Elaine and Aaron Cohen. *Automation, Space Management and Productivity: A Guide for Librarians.* New York: R. R. Bowker, 1981.

Cohen, Elaine. "Designing Libraries to Sell Services" *Wilson Library Bulletin,* November 1980, 190–95.

"Daylighting: Six Aalto Libraries." *The AIA Journal,* June 1983, 58–70.

DeChiara, Joseph, and John Callender. *Time Saver Standards for Building Types.* 2d ed. New York: McGraw-Hill, 1980.

Draper, James, and James Brooks. *Interior Design for Libraries.* Chicago: American Library Assn., 1979.

Ellsworth, Ralph E. "ABC's of Remodeling/Enlarging an Academic Library Building: A Personal Statement." *Journal of Academic Librarianship* 7 (January 1982):334–43.

Ellsworth, Ralph E. *Planning the College and University Library Building: A Book for Campus Planners and Architects.* Boulder, Colo.: Pruet Press, 1968.

Fraley, Ruth A., and Carol Lee Anderson. *Library Space Planning.* New York: Neal-Schuman, 1985.

Galvin, Hoyt R. "Additional Remodeling/Renovation Projects." *Library Journal Special Report #1: Library Space Planning,* 1976.

Garecki, Drahoslav. *Compact Library Shelving.* Translated by Stanislav Rehak. Chicago: American Library Assn., 1968.

Gore, Daniel, ed. *Farewell to Alexandria: Solutions to Space, Growth, and Performance Problems of Libraries.* Westport, Conn.: Greenwood Press, 1976.

Hall, Richard B. "Library Space Utilization Methodology." *Library Journal* 103 (June 1979):2379–83.

Haymond, Jay. "Adaptive Reuse of Old Buildings for Archives." *American Archivist* 45 (Winter 1982):11–18.

Jeffs, Joseph E. "Saving Space, Energy, and Money with Mobile Compact Shelving: Georgetown University." *Library Journal Special Report #1: Library Space Planning*, 1976.

Jones, Harold D. "Recent Trends in West German University Library Building Planning." *College and Research Libraries* 42 (September 1981):461–69.

Langmead, Stephen, and Margaret Beckman. *New Library Design: Guidelines to Planning Academic Library Buildings*. New York: John Wiley and Sons, 1970.

Lieberfeld, Lawrence. "Research Notes: The Curious Case of the Library Building." *College and Research Libraries* 44 (July 1983):277–82.

Library Planning, Bookstacks, and Shelving with Contributions from the Architects and Librarians' Points of View. Jersey City, N.J.: Snead and Company Ironworks, 1915.

Lushington, Nolan, and Willis N. Mills, Jr. *Libraries Designed for Users*. Syracuse, N.Y.: Gaylord, 1979.

Markwick, Emily. *A Librarian Plans a Library*. London: Library Association, 1971.

Martin, Jess A. "Planning the New NIH Research Library." *Special Libraries* 59 (January 1968):30–38.

Mason, Ellsworth. *Mason on Library Buildings*. Metuchen, N.J.: Scarecrow Press, 1980.

Metcalf, Keyes. *Library Lighting*. Washington, D.C.: Association of Research Libraries, 1970.

Metcalf, Keyes. *Planning Academic and Research Library Buildings*. New York: McGraw-Hill, 1965.

Metcalf, Keyes. "Problems of Renovating an Existing Library Building." *Running out of Space—What Are the Alternatives?* Edited by Gloria Novak. Chicago: American Library Assn., 1978.

Miller, Ellen G. " 'Why' Comes before 'How' ": Planning for Automation in the Real World." *Technicalities* 2 (June 1982): 13–16.

Mount, Ellis, ed. "Planning the Special Library." SLA Monograph, no. 4. New York: Special Libraries Association, 1972.

Myller, Rolf. *The Design of the Small Public Library*. New York: Bowker, 1966.

Nwafor, B. U. "The Spine or the Heart: The University of Jos in Search of a Library Building Model." *College and Research Libraries* 42 (September 1981): 447–55.

Office of Management Studies. *Building Renovation in ARL Libraries.* Spec Flyer, #97. Washington, D. C.: Association of Research Libraries, September 1983.

Office of the Executive Director of University-Wide Library Planning. *The University of California Libraries: A Plan for Development, 1978–1988.* Berkeley: System Wide Administration University of California, 1977.

Pierce, William S. *Furnishing the Library Interior.* New York: Marcel Dekker, 1980.

Prospect, Robert. "Human Needs and Working Places." *Running out of Space—What are the Alternatives?* Edited by Gloria Novak. Chicago: American Library Assn., 1978.

Recommended Minimum Standards for Virginia Public Libraries. Richmond: Virginia State Library, 1978.

Schell, Hal B., ed. *Reader on the Library Building.* Englewood, Calif.: Microcard Edition Books, 1975.

Shaw, Robert J., ed. *Libraries: Building for the Future.* Chicago: American Library Assn., 1967.

Swartz, Philip. "Demand-Adjusted Shelf Availability Parameters: A Second Look." *College and Research Libraries* 44 (July 1983): 210–19.

Thompson, Godfrey. *Planning and Design of Library Buildings.* 2d ed. New York: Nichols Publishing Co., 1977.

Tilton, Edward L. "Library Planning." *Architectural Forum* 47 (December 1927):497–506.

Wheeler, Joseph L., and Alfred Morton Githens. *The American Public Library Building: Its Planning and Design with Special Reference to its Administration and Service.* New York: Charles Scribner's Sons, 1941.

INDEX

A

Academic libraries, New York State, guidelines for assessing adequacy of, 92–94
Acoustic control, microform area, 49
Acquisition decisions, basis of, 27
Air conditioning system, 38, 48
Air flow, 38
Apple II, 17
Architects
  qualified, 103
  role of, 104
Association of Research Libraries study, 45
Attitude, 102
Audio reproduction, high quality, 60
Automation, 5–6
  introduction of, 26
  library systems, *see* Library automation

B

Banks, optical media use, 66
Bell Operating Companies, 14
Bibliofile, 62, 65
Bibliographic data bases, 15
Bibliographic utilities, 8–9
  nonprofit, vs. commercial suppliers of records, 9–11
Boolean searching, 8
BRUNET (Brown University system), 22
BTU output, 38

C

California State University and Colleges (CSUC) space formula, 91
Carrells, 50–51, 69, 89, 102
  design of, 109
  major advantage of, 51
  patron seating calculation, 107–108
CD-ROM (compact disc read-only memory), 9, 10, 11, 61–63, 68
  disk storage capacity, 62
  major application of, 61
  shared cataloging, 27
Central site hardware, 30–31
Clapp-Jordan Formula, 92
CL-Medline, 64
Closed access systems, 84–85
CLSI, 64
CLSI "dumb label" format, 7
Coaxial cable, 25
Codabar symbology, 7
Collection factors, 93
Compact disc, 60–61
Compact shelving, 81, 82–84
  three modes of, 83
Compact storage, 81–88
  costs, 87
  floor loading, 86
  lighting, 86–87
  shelving, 82–84
  space requirements, 88
Compatibility, digital machines, 79–80
Computer Assisted Retrieval (CAR), 46
Computer room, 104–105
Computer-to-computer communication, 13–14

Console, electrical requirements, 35
Consultants
    qualified, 103
    role of, 104
Consultative Committee on International Telephone and Telegraph (CCITT), 78
Copy resolution, 75
Copyright, 24, 102
Costs
    compact storage, 87
    data communication, 24

D

Data base
    building local, 17–20
    full-text, 15
    reference, 15
    remote searching, 14–16
    source, 15
Data cables, installing, 36–37
Data communications, costs as factor in technology use, 24–25
Data Resources Inc. (DRI), 15
Dehumidifiers, 48–49
Delivery services
    alternatives, 73
    cost-efficient, 72–73
    rapid, 73
DIALOG, 14
Digital dumps, 58
Digitally encoded videodiscs, 9–10
Digitial telefacsimile, 74–75
    equipment, 110
Direct patron access, 53
Disk drives, electrical requirements, 35
Disk packs, storage, 31–32
Documentation, storage, 33
Document feeding, 76–77
DRAW (direct-read-after-write), 10, 11, 63, 66

E

Electrical/telecommunications requirements, 34–39
    central site, 34–36
    line conditioner, 35–36
    power lines, 34–35

remote peripherals, 36–37
subpanel box, 35
Environmental conditions, automated systems, 38–39

F

Fiber optics, 25
Filing systems
    compact, 84
    mobile, 81
Fire protection, 39
Flexibility, 103
    work space, 90
Floor loading, 86, 106–107
Formulas
    reliance on, 98
    revisions required, 98–99
    space planning, 89–100
Free space, 31
Furniture selection, 109

G

Glare, 110
GRC, 10
Grolier Electronic Encyclopedia, 11

H

Halon fire extinguishers, 39
Hard copy, moving, 25–26
Holmes, Donald C., 45
Humidity, 38, 48

I

IBM PC, 17
IIT Research Institute (IITRI), 58
IITR Videodisc Production System (IVPS), 58
Illinois University Library space formula, 91–92
ILL subsystems, 12
Information
    access from home or office, 20
    hard-copy, 25–26
Information sharing, 47
Information Systems Consultants Inc., 11, 42
Insurance companies, optial media use, 66

Interfacing, 13–14
  standards for, 13
Interlibrary loan, 9
  cost-efficient material delivery,
    72–73
InterRoyal, 86

K

Kardex, 84
Key-word searching, 8
Kurzweil Computer Products, 18
Kurzweil Data Entry Machine
    (KDEM), 18
  complex printed material,
    throughput rate, 19
  limitations to, 19

L

LaserData, 59
Layout
  library computer room, 39–40
  microform area, 50
LC MARC data base, 58, 62
Lektriever, 84, 85
Library automation
  electrical/telecommunication re-
    quirements, 34–37
  fire protection, 39
  layout, 39–40
  space requirements, 29–30
Library of Congress, 57
  optical digital disk investigation,
    64–65
Library of Congress Network Ad-
    visory Committee, 12
Library Corporation, 10, 65
Library staff
  space for, 90
  work areas, 108–109
Library Systems & Services Inc.,
    10, 58
Licensing, 24
Lighting, 86–87
Linear feet, conversion to square
    feet, 97–98
Linked Systems Project, 13
Lister Hill National Center for
    Biomedical Communications,
    59
Local area networks (LANs), 20–
    22

applications, 21
characteristics, 20–21
machines linked by, 21–22
Lundia (open access system), 85

M

MAGIC (software package), 15
MARC editing, 8
Maryland Council for Higher Edu-
    cation, 95–97
Micro-based workstations, 27, 33,
    68, 103
  provision for, 105
Microform, 41–54
  area layout, 50
  changing usage patterns, 46–48
  conversion study results, 42–44
  cost data, 43–44
  payback period for conversion,
    44–45
  printing area, 52
  reading area, 50–51
  reducing resistance to, 45–46
  space requirements, 48–50
  as space saving technique, 107
  staff area, 53–54
  storage area, 52–53
Micros as workstations, 17
Microwave, 25
Minicomputers, 6, 7
MiniMARC cataloging support
    system, 58
Mobile shelving, see Compact
    shelving
Modems, 25
Multiplexors, 25
Multiuser systems, 7
  optical digital disk use, 69

N

National Commission on Libraries,
    1977
  study of, 13
Networks
  local area (LANs), 20–22
  shared cataloging, 8
  state and regional, 11–12
Nippon Electric Company (NEC),
    75, 78
NISO (National Information Stan-
    dards Organization), 13